尾田栄一郎

Reader: Who're you calling a hijacker? Divine retribution to the manga creator who doesn't trust his readers. Switch...on. Click. Kokoro bra-drop in 10...9...8...7...6...5...4...3...2...1... **PLOP!** And now for the comic.

--Kaimori

Oda: Ahhhhhh! Volume 48 is now starting!

-Eiichiro Oda, 2007

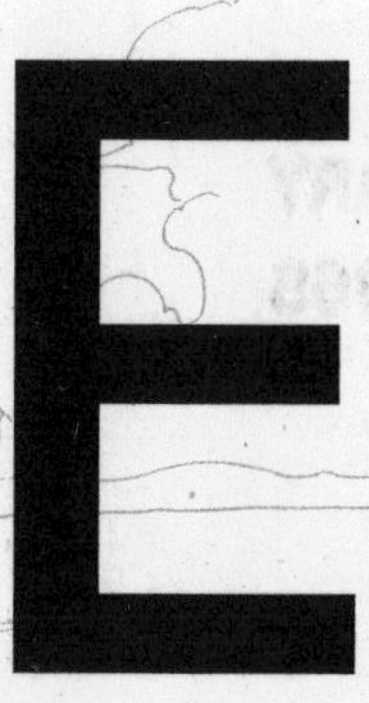

iichiro Oda began his manga career at the age of 17, when his one-shot cowboy manga **Wanted!** won second place in the coveted Tezuka manga awards. Oda went on to work as an assistant to some of the biggest manga artists in the industry, including Nobuhiro Watsuki, before winning the Hop Step Award for new artists. His pirate adventure **One Piece**, which debuted in **Weekly Shonen Jump** in 1997, quickly became one of the most popular manga in Japan.

ONE PIECE VOL. 48
THRILLER BARK PART 3

SHONEN JUMP Manga Edition

STORY AND ART BY EIICHIRO ODA

English Adaptation/Jason Thompson
Translation/Labaaman, HC Language Solutions, Inc.
Touch-up Art & Lettering/HudsonYards
Design/Sean Lee
Supervising Editor/Alexis Kirsch
Editor/Megan Bates

Printed in the U.S.A.

Published by VIZ Media, LLC
P.O. Box 77010
San Francisco, CA 94107

10 9 8
First printing, May 2010
Eighth printing, December 2016

www.viz.com

PARENTAL ADVISORY
ONE PIECE is rated T for Teen and is recommended for ages 13 and up. This volume contains fantasy violence and tobacco usage.

ratings.viz.com

www.shonenjump.com

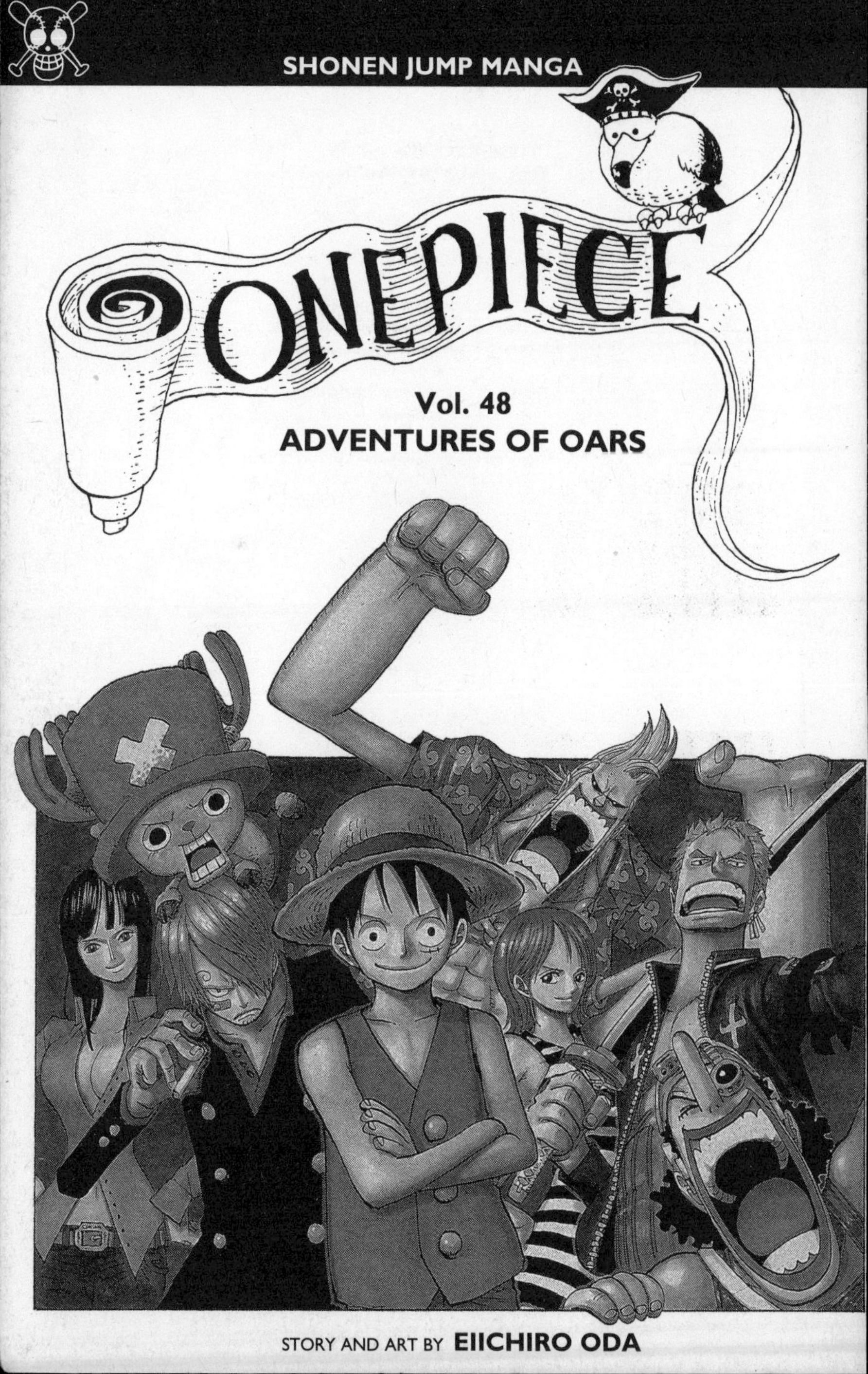
SHONEN JUMP MANGA
ONE PIECE
Vol. 48
ADVENTURES OF OARS
STORY AND ART BY EIICHIRO ODA

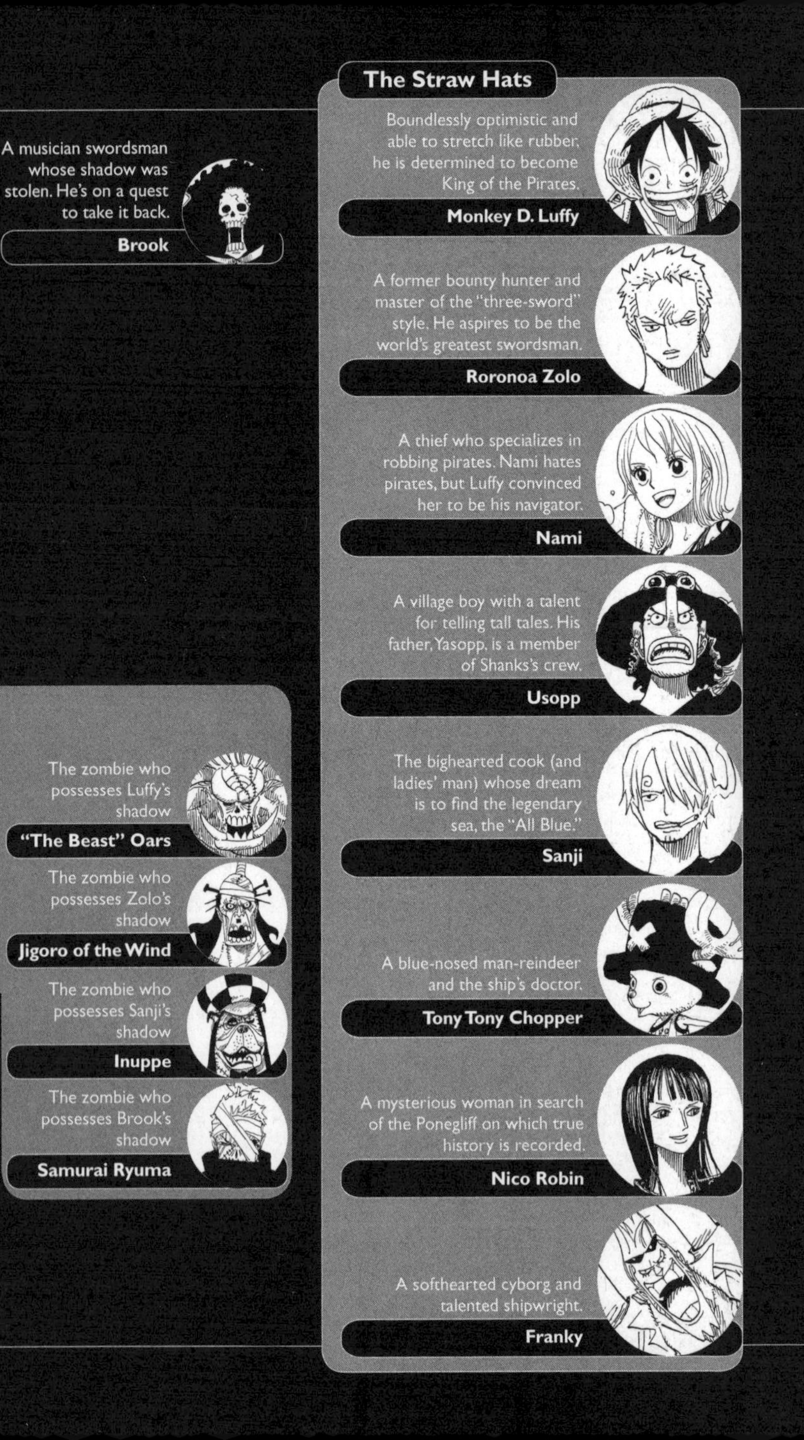
The Straw Hats
Boundlessly optimistic and able to stretch like rubber, he is determined to become King of the Pirates.
Monkey D. Luffy
A former bounty hunter and master of the "three-sword" style. He aspires to be the world's greatest swordsman.
Roronoa Zolo
A thief who specializes in robbing pirates. Nami hates pirates, but Luffy convinced her to be his navigator.
Nami
A village boy with a talent for telling tall tales. His father, Yasopp, is a member of Shanks's crew.
Usopp
The bighearted cook (and ladies' man) whose dream is to find the legendary sea, the "All Blue."
Sanji
A blue-nosed man-reindeer and the ship's doctor.
Tony Tony Chopper
A mysterious woman in search of the Poneglyph on which true history is recorded.
Nico Robin
A softhearted cyborg and talented shipwright.
Franky
A musician swordsman whose shadow was stolen. He's on a quest to take it back.
Brook
The zombie who possesses Luffy's shadow
"The Beast" Oars
The zombie who possesses Zolo's shadow
Jigoro of the Wind
The zombie who possesses Sanji's shadow
Inuppe
The zombie who possesses Brook's shadow
Samurai Ryuma

THE STORY OF ONE PIECE

Volume 48

Monkey D. Luffy started out as just a kid with a dream—to become the greatest pirate in history! Stirred by the tales of pirate "Red-Haired" Shanks, Luffy vowed to become a pirate himself. That was before the enchanted Devil Fruit gave Luffy the power to stretch like rubber, at the cost of being unable to swim—a serious handicap for an aspiring sea dog. Undeterred, Luffy set out to sea and recruited some crewmates—master swordsman Zolo; treasure-hunting thief Nami; lying sharpshooter Usopp; the high-kicking chef Sanji; Chopper, the walkin' talkin' reindeer doctor; the mysterious archaeologist Robin; and cyborg shipwright Franky.

Luffy and crew have just directed their new vessel, the *Thousand Sunny*, toward Fish-Man Island on the Grand Line when they are caught in a storm and find themselves adrift in the perpetual fogs of the Florian Triangle. There they encounter Brook, a jovial skeleton with no shadow. Suddenly, the ship is pulled into the waters around Thriller Bark, a mysterious place where zombies roam. Nami is kidnapped by a zombie general with romantic designs, while Gecko Moria—the warlord who took Brook's shadow—also steals the shadows of Zolo, Sanji and Luffy. Working with the immoral Dr. Hogback, he creates the ultimate zombie warrior using Luffy's shadow! Meanwhile, Franky learns about the skeleton Brook's unfulfilled vow to this friend Laboon. The group reunites on their ship and makes plans to return to Thriller Bark to retake their stolen shadows, save Nami from an unwanted marriage, and help Brook make good on his promise!

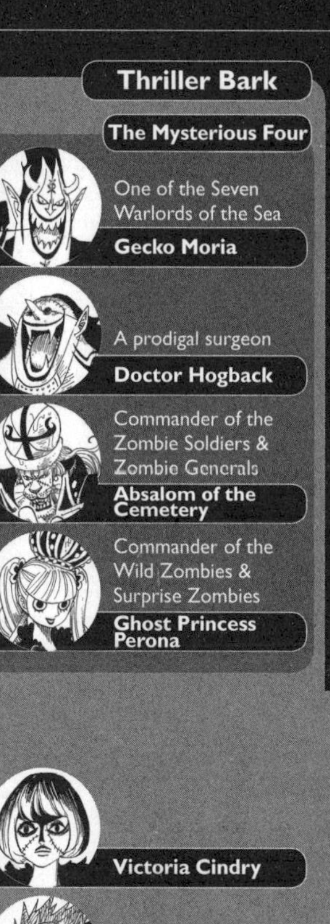

A pirate that Luffy idolizes. Shanks gave Luffy his trademark straw hat.

"Red-Haired" Shanks

Vol. 48
Adventures of Oars

CONTENTS

Chapter 460: CONQUEST BEFORE DAWN!

ENERU'S GREAT SPACE MISSION, VOL. 26:
"INSOLENCE!!"

BUT IT MIGHT BE REALLY HARD...
...TO FIND THE ZOMBIES WHO HAVE OUR SHADOWS.
RMBB...
LUFFY'S ZOMBIE IS HUGE--TWICE AS BIG AS A GIANT!
I DON'T EVEN KNOW IF YOU'LL BE ABLE TO DEFEAT IT!
YOU DON'T HAVE TO LOOK FOR THE ZOMBIES.
BUT I DO WANT TO TAKE A LOOK AT MINE.
?
WHAT ARE YOU TALKING ABOUT? THE WAY THINGS ARE WE'LL NEVER BE ABLE TO STEP IN THE SUN AGAIN.
DON'T YOU REMEMBER...
...WHAT THAT ZOMBIE DUDE SAID?
YOU GUYS CAN DEFEAT MORIA!
IF WE BEAT GECKO MORIA, EVERYONE'S SHADOW WILL COME BACK!
?!!

...!!
...
HE DID SAY THAT.
LUFFY HAS A WAY OF GETTING RIGHT TO THE POINT...
?
AND MORIA'S AT THE TOP OF THOSE STAIRS, RIGHT?
WHOA! YEAH!!
THRILLER BAR
SO ANYWAY...
I'M GOING TO GO BEAT UP MORIA!
THE SHADOWS WILL ALL COME BACK AFTER THAT.
SANJI, YOU'LL TAKE CARE OF NAMI, RIGHT?
OF COURSE!!
I DON'T CARE IF HE'S INVISIBLE OR INDIVISIBLE! I'LL KICK HIM SO HARD HE FLIES ABOVE THE FOGLINE!!!
BWOOOF!!!
I WON'T LET HIM MARRY HER!!

I FORGOT TO MENTION THIS, BUT THAT INVISIBLE GUY SAW NAMI NAKED IN THE BATH.
GRAAAH
WHAAAT ?!
THAT CREEP!
AAAAAAAAAAAAA
BWOOF
STOP PROVOKING HIM.
HE'S ABOUT TO MUTATE.
I DO FEEL RESPONSIBLE FOR LETTING THEM TAKE NAMI AWAY RIGHT BEFORE MY EYES.
I'M GOING WITH SANJI!
BESIDES, I NEVER WANT TO SEE ONE OF THE SEVEN WARLORDS EVER AGAIN!!
I'M WORRIED ABOUT THE SKELETON'S BATTLE, SO I'LL GO CHECK UP ON HIM!
IF STRAW HAT BEATS UP MORIA FIRST, THAT'LL BE RESOLVED TOO.
FWIK...!
BUT IF ANYTHING HAPPENS TO HIM BEFORE HE GETS HIS SHADOW BACK, IT'LL BE HORRIBLE.
I'LL GO WITH YOU, FRANKY.
I WANT TO SEE HOW STRONG THAT LEGENDARY SAMURAI ZOMBIE IS.
TMP

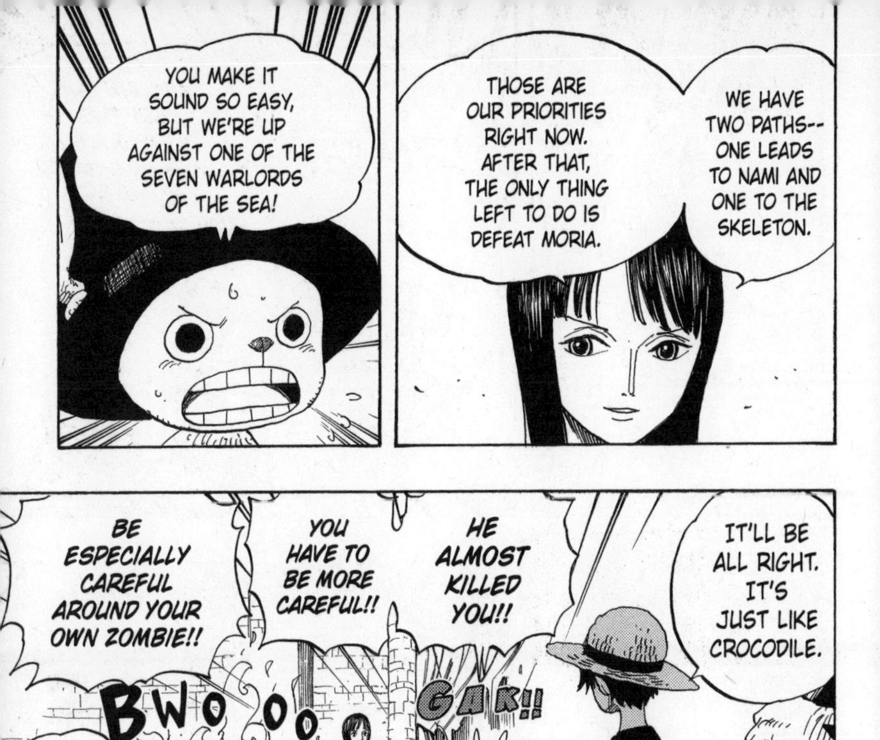

WE HAVE TWO PATHS-- ONE LEADS TO NAMI AND ONE TO THE SKELETON.
THOSE ARE OUR PRIORITIES RIGHT NOW. AFTER THAT, THE ONLY THING LEFT TO DO IS DEFEAT MORIA.
YOU MAKE IT SOUND SO EASY, BUT WE'RE UP AGAINST ONE OF THE SEVEN WARLORDS OF THE SEA!
IT'LL BE ALL RIGHT. IT'S JUST LIKE CROCODILE.
HE ALMOST KILLED YOU!!
YOU HAVE TO BE MORE CAREFUL!!
BE ESPECIALLY CAREFUL AROUND YOUR OWN ZOMBIE!!
GAK!!
BWOOO
ALL RIGHT, ALREADY.

HERE, YOU GUYS...
EACH OF YOU TAKE A BAG.
HM?
THIS IS MY SPECIAL ZOMBIE DEATH SALT BALL!!
SO THIS IS WHAT YOU WERE WORKING ON. NICE JOB.
FLUP
NONE OF YOU REALLY UNDERSTAND THE CONCEPT OF DANGER.
LET ME TELL YOU ONE THING!

NO MATTER HOW THICK THE FOG LIES ON THESE WATERS...
...THERE'S NO GUARANTEE THAT THE SUN WON'T SHINE THROUGH.
WE'RE ONLY SAFE NOW BECAUSE IT'S NIGHT.
IN OTHER WORDS, YOU SHOULD ASSUME THAT SUNRISE WILL BE OUR FINAL DEADLINE!
YEAH!!
IT'LL SUCK IF WE DON'T GET ANYTHING TO EAT UNTIL SUNRISE!!
THEY'LL PAY FOR PICKING A FIGHT WITH US!!
I'LL MAKE YOU REGRET IT, GECKO MORIA!!!
WE'LL TAKE BACK THE FOOD THEY STOLE AND TAKE THEIRS TOO. BEFORE SUNRISE!!
RAAAAH!!
UH... I WAS TALKING ABOUT GETTING BACK THE SHADOWS!!!
NAMI!!!!!
BWOO
LET'S GO.
YEAH!!
YOU GUYS ARE CRAZY!!!

WOW !!!
SO THIS PLACE IS A SHIP!!
KREEK...
KREEK...
DOOM!!
FLIT
...
THE OCEAN VIEW SUCKS...
RM RM RM RM
BUT MY OUTLOOK ON MY OWN LIFE IS AWESOME!
OKAY! I'M GOING TO TAKE THIS SHIP AND BECOME THE PIRATE KING!
RM RM...
RM RM
THRILLER BARK
THRILLER BARK
WHERE IS OARS?
...
FLIIIT

HE'S CLIMBED ON TOP OF THE MAST, MASTER.
MASTER! WITH THAT HUGE ZOMBIE WALKING AROUND...
...WE CAN'T EVEN DO THE FEVER DANCE IN PEACE!
THAT GUY IS ROTTEN DANGEROUS!
WHOOSH
IT'LL BE FINE. IT'S ONLY A MATTER OF TIME.
WITH OARS AROUND...
...WE CAN STEAL THE SHADOWS OF EVEN STRONGER WARRIORS...
...AND CREATE EVEN MORE TOP-NOTCH ZOMBIES! KI SHI SHI!
LOOKS LIKE WE'LL BE NEEDING MORE POWERFUL MARIONETTES, HOGBACK.
I'LL GET RIGHT ON IT. FO HO HO!
DR. HOGBACK!!
WE HAVE A PROBLEM! THE PIRATES...
WHAT'S THE MATTER, HILDON?
FLUP
FLUP
FLUP

THE THREE WHOSE SHADOWS WE JUST TOOK AWAKENED ON THEIR SHIP, AND THEY'RE ON THEIR WAY BACK!
FLUP FLUP
WHAT?! THEY JUST HAD THEIR SHADOWS TAKEN--IT'S IMPOSSI-BLE FOR THEM TO WAKE UP THIS SOON!!
IT SEEMS THEY WERE BEATEN AWAKE BY THE OTHER CREW MEMBERS!!
...
?!
AND THEY SEEM TO BE CONNECTED WITH THE HUMMING SWORDSMAN...
SO THEY MUST BE GETTING ALL OF THEIR IN-FORMATION FROM HIM!!
...
BASICALLY, BY NOW THOSE PI-RATES...
...MUST ALL KNOW HOW TO PURIFY ZOMBIES!
WHAT?!
THE ZOMBIES ARE NOW IN COMPLETE FEAR OF THE PIRATES...
RMRMRM RM...
EEEK
EEE
AAAH
...AND THEY'RE RUNNING AROUND IN A FRENZY!!!
...!!

THE WILD ZOMBIES, SURPRISE ZOMBIES AND ZOMBIE SOLDIERS...
...NONE OF THEM STAND A CHANCE, EVEN *WITHOUT* SALT!
SEND THE ZOMBIE GENERALS.
THEY SHOULD BE ABLE TO BEAT THE PIRATES AND AVOID THE SALT!
WHAT IS ABSALOM DOING RIGHT NOW?
WELL...
HIS WEDDING IS JUST STARTING...
BUZZ
BUZZ
FIDDLE
FIDDLE
...AND, UH, MOST OF THE ZOMBIE GENERALS ARE...
...PARTICIPATING IN THE CEREMONY RIGHT NOW.
WHAT IS THAT IDIOT DOING?!
OH, YES. THE BANQUET WILL BE IN ONE HOUR...
...AND HE WANTS YOU TO DO YOUR SPECIAL TUMMY DANCE TO LIVEN UP THE PARTY.
HMM. IT'S TRUE THAT A WEDDING IS THE MOST MEMORABLE EVENT OF A LIFETIME. MY PERFORMANCE WILL BE SURE TO MAKE IT ALL THE MORE...
THIS IS NO TIME TO DANCE !!!
GRAH!!!

HAVE HIM STOP THE WEDDING, RIGHT AWAY!!!
BUT I'M JUST AN ORDINARY ZOMBIE. I CAN'T TELL MASTER ABSALOM WHAT TO DO.
HORO HORO HORO!
YOU DON'T NEED TO RELY ON THOSE BEASTS.
ALL I HAVE TO DO IS WEAKEN THE ENEMIES WITH MY GHOSTS...
...THEN THE ZOMBIE SOLDIERS SHOULD BE ABLE TO CAPTURE THEM.
JUST BECAUSE THEY DISCOVERED THE ZOMBIES' WEAKNESS DOESN'T MEAN IT'S TIME TO PANIC.
I'LL CAPTURE THEM AND SEND THEM HERE.
PREPARE ENOUGH MARIONETTES TO RECEIVE THE SHADOWS OF THE REMAINING PIRATES!
KLIK KLIK
I'LL BE IN MY ROOM.
LET'S GO, KUMACY!
OH...
SHE'S RIGHT. YOU CAN REALLY DEPEND ON HER IN TIMES LIKE THESE. IT'S JUST AS YOU'D EXPECT FROM THE GHOST PRINCESS.
YOU COULD TAKE A LESSON FROM KUMACY.

IT IS GOING TO BE ALL RIGHT, MASTER MORIA.
FLUP FLUP...
SHLUMP
OH REALLY...
WELL, THIS IS NO FUN AT ALL.
OH, PLEASE. YOU PROBABLY WEREN'T PLANNING TO HELP OUT ANYWAY.

I'M GOING TO STAY HERE A LITTLE LONGER...
...BECAUSE I WANT TO PLAY WITH OARS A BIT.
THEN I HAVE ONE REQUEST.
BECAUSE THAT IDIOT ABSALOM IS INDISPOSED...
...PLEASE ALLOW ME TO COMMAND TWO ZOMBIES.

AHHHH!
KRAKA BOOM!!

WHERE IS MORIA ?!!
GIVE ME BACK MY FOOD!!!
AHHH!!
AHHHH!
WHO'S THE CREEP WHO PEEPED AT NAMI IN THE BATHTUB?!
WHERE ARE YOU? GET OUT HERE!!!
AAAHA
AAAH
LOOKS LIKE THEY DON'T NEED THE SALT YET.
I GUESS THEY DON'T CARE ABOUT THE SHADOWS!
TMP TMP TMP
THERE'S ANGER IN THEIR HEARTS.
THERE ARE FIVE OF THEM, AND THEY'RE COMING TOWARD THE DANCE HALL!!
YEEK

AND TWO MORE ON THE BOTTOM BRIDGE!
AAAH
To Moria in the Dance Hall
Luffy
Sanji
Usopp
Chopper
Robin
To Perona's RooM
Zolo
Franky
EEK
WAH
EEK
WAH
WE CAN'T FEND THEM ALL OFF!!
SMASH!!
WAAAH!!
JUST THINKING ABOUT HOW THESE WEAK-LINGS CAPTURED ME BEFORE...
...MAKES ME MORE ANGRY!!!
HEY, I'M THE ONE WHO FREED YOU.
YOU CAN CALL ME "BIG BROTHER" IF YOU WANT.
NEVER!!

OH NO...!!
WHAT?! WHAT HAPPENED?!
WHOA! LUFFY!! SANJI!!
WHAT HAPPENED?!
I'M FINISHED. IF I GET REBORN...
...I WANT TO COME BACK AS A WORM.
MY EYEBROWS ARE SO CURLY...
...I WISH I WERE DEAD.
GLOOM...
GOT YOU!!
WAP!!
BOTH OF THEM GOT CAUGHT!! WHY?!
IT'S BECAUSE OF THOSE GHOSTS! THEY MAKE WHOMEVER THEY TOUCH EXTREMELY DEPRESSED.
AND WE DON'T HAVE ANY WAY TO COUNTER IT RIGHT NOW!
NEGATIVE THOUGHTS
...!!
GRAAA
LEAD STAR!!
WHAK!!
GAH!!
HURRY! WE DON'T HAVE ANY CHOICE BUT TO RUN!
IF WE END UP LIKE THAT, WE'RE ALL FINISHED!
AGH! IF WE ALL GET CAUGHT, NO ONE CAN BE SAVED!!
NEGATIVE THOUGHTS
LET'S SET SAIL!
SWOOO

WHOOPS!
AASH!!

KR
AAAHH !!!
KRMBB
?!!
WE'RE FALLING!!
USOPP!!
RM RM RM RM RM
SANJI!!
RM RM
KRMB
RM RM RM
!!!
KRMB...
RM RM RM... RM
AAAAH
KRAK
KRAK

WHA?!
HUFF...
?
HUFF
ASIDE FROM WHAT HAPPENED TO THESE TWO...
...WHAT'S GOING ON?
WHAT... WHAT HAPPENED?!
...
WAS THAT... NO, IT CAN'T BE!
HUFF
HUFF
BUT THAT SURPRISED ME! THE STAIRS JUST DISAPPEARED!
KRMBB...
ALL THE ZOMBIES...
...AND USOPP AND SANJI...
HUFF
KRMBB...
HUFF
KOFF... WHAT JUST HAPPENED?!
HUPP...
EVERY-ONE...
DOOOOM
...FELL.
KRMB
WOOOOOOO...!!
THAT'S LUFFY'S ...

OUR PATH WAS SUDDENLY BLOCKED.
WHAT IS THIS WALL?!
TWITCH...!
OW! WHAT WAS THAT?!
SKREK...!!
?!!!
HMPH!
HUH? THIS ISN'T STONE!
JAB!!
WEAPONS LEFT!!!
BAM!!
WHAT ARE YOU TWO DOING?!
THE WALL JUST CAME DOWN ON US.
THAT ISN'T A WALL, IDIOT!
... ZOMBIE !!!
?!!
DOOM!!
WHAAT ?!!

Reader: Ding dong! Delivery! Delivering the dirty mag that you ordered the other day! If you don't let me start the Question Corner, I won't give you this dirty mag! What?! You don't care and you just want the dirty mag?! Then I get to start it, right?! Great! ***Starting the Question Corner!!!*** Okay, as promised, here's your dirty mag!

--Tani-san

Oda: Yup. I love smut more than food, more than starting the Question Corner... Oh, look, this is a good issue too. I just love the curves on this girl. Whoa! Look at those! **What kind of pervert do you think I am?!** Stop it! That's so not me!

Q: Hello, Odacchi. I have a question… Will you hear me out? Are you sure? Thanks! So the Straw Hat Pirates sing the song "Family." One of the lyrics is "We're not just acquaintances, we're not just friends. We are family!" So if Luffy and the crew are a family (among the Straw Hats), who's the dad and who's the mom?

--Anonymous

A: I heard "Family" when it aired on TV. It might be the most well known of all the character songs. It's also one of my favorite tunes. Now, to answer your question, I think it's like this: Dad: Franky (street punk), Mother: Robin, Eldest Son: Zolo, Second Son: Sanji (delinquent), Eldest Daughter: Nami, Third Son: Usopp, Fourth Son: Luffy, Baby Brother: Chopper

Q: Please tell us "Fire Fist" Ace's height and weight! By the way, I want his birthday to be January 1. What do you think?

--AI♡

A: I guess you could say he's like the Ace in a deck of cards, so January 1 would be fine. And his height is about 185 cm.

Chapter 461:
GHOST BUSTER

ENERU'S GREAT SPACE MISSION, VOL. 27:
"GRATITUDE FOR AVENGING THE DOCTOR"

THRILLER BARK, *MAST MANSION*

Luffy Chopper Robin

Zolo Franky Sanji Usopp

Oars

● Moria's Dance Hall
● Moria's Bedroom
● Perona's Room
● Wonder Garden

USOPP AND SANJI FELL DOWN BACK THERE.

ARE YOU GOING TO LEAVE THEM?

YEAH. THEY'LL BE FINE!

WE HAVE TO GET TO MORIA BEFORE HE MOVES.

I'M GOING TO FIND THAT GIANT ONION GUY AND BEAT HIM UP!

ALL RIGHT. THAT'S THE QUICKEST WAY TO END ALL OF THIS!

THAT'S THE ENTRANCE TO THE DANCE HALL WHERE YOUR SHADOW WAS TAKEN!

THERE'S A FREEZER FURTHER IN-- THAT'S THE LAST PLACE WE SAW MORIA!

ALL RIGHT!
!
?!
HEY...
DOOM!!
WHOA! IT'S YOU!
I THOUGHT PERONA GOT TO YOU ALREADY!

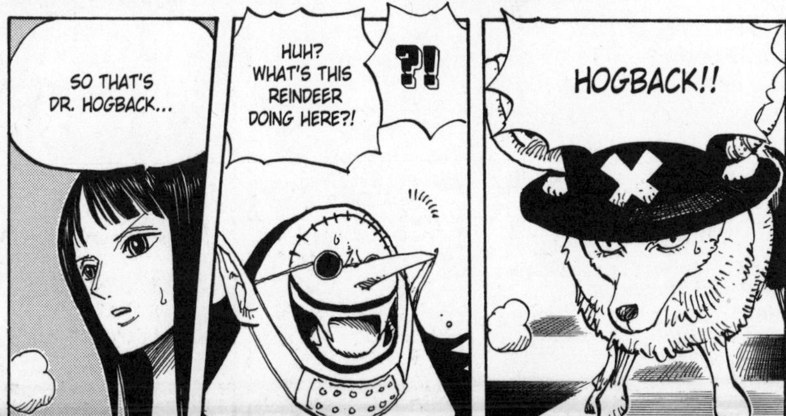
HOGBACK!!
?!
HUH? WHAT'S THIS REINDEER DOING HERE?!
SO THAT'S DR. HOGBACK...

YOU'RE THE GUY WHO WORKS WITH MORIA! SHOULD I BEAT HIM UP TOO?!
WIP WIP!!
W-WAIT!
WAIT, LUFFY!!!
LET ME TAKE CARE OF HIM.
...!!
YOU SEE THAT DOOR IN THE BACK? THAT'S THE FREEZER!
GO ON WITHOUT ME!!!
OKAY!
HMPH.
HOW DARE YOU TRY TO GET TO MASTER MORIA WITHOUT FIGHTING ME FIRST!
CINDRY! GET THEM!
CLANK...!!
YES.

ONE! TWO!
KRASH!! KRASH!!
WHOA! DISHES ?!!
THREE...
?!!
WAPP
SWP
SWP
LUFFY...
...GO ON WITHOUT US.
YEAH!
...!!
THANKS, ROBIN!
TMP TMP!!
HM?! WHAT HAPPENED, CINDRY?!
WAIT! STRAW HAT LUFFY!
TMP TMP TMP...
HOG-BACK!!!
!!

I'VE LOST...
...ALL RESPECT FOR YOU!!!
YOU DON'T DESERVE TO BE CALLED A DOCTOR!!
OH, FO HO HO. I DIDN'T RECOGNIZE YOU, DR. CHOPPER.
SO YOU'RE A ZOAN-TYPE DEVIL FRUIT USER. I KNEW YOU WERE A STRANGE CREATURE.
I DON'T KNOW HOW YOU ESCAPED AFTER BEING CARRIED THROUGH PERONA'S GARDEN...
...BUT NOW THAT WE'VE MET HERE, I WILL NOT LET YOU GO! YOUR SHADOW WILL BE MINE!!!
...
NO...
INSTEAD...
...WHY DON'T I TURN YOU INTO A MARI-ONETTE, AFTER YOU'VE BEEN KILLED...
...AT THEIR HANDS?
?!!
KLAK
KLUNK...

THIS HALL...
...IS WAY LONGER THAN I THOUGHT!
TMP TMP TMP TMP TMP...!!
HUFF
HUFF... HUFF... ALL RIGHT. I'M OUT!
HUFF
WHAT IS THIS PLACE?!
HUFF
?
SHKKK...!!
WOOOOO...
HEY!
THERE YOU ARE!!!
YO.
IT'S YOU...
RMRM
RMRM...

IT'S HUGE!!!
BRIDGE TO PERONA'S ROOM
...
KRMB KRMBB...
IS IT SOME KIND OF DEMON LORD?! I'VE NEVER SEEN A GIANT *THIS* BIG!!
THIS IS THE ZOMBIE?!
THIS IS...
...LUFFY?!
IT'S ALL OVER! IT'S GONNA KILL US!!!

RM
RM
RM...
?!
AAAH !!!
GRAP!!
KRMBB...
GAH! WHAT IS IT TRYING TO DO?!
THUMP!!
OH.
THAT FITS JUST RIGHT!

YEAH! THIS IS MORE LIKE IT!!
NOW I'M GOING TO BE THE ROTTEN PIRATE KING!
DOMP DOMP...
MAN, I FREAKED OUT WHEN THAT BUILDING FELL DOWN.
?!
HUH. HE DIDN'T EVEN NOTICE US.
HE TALKS JUST LIKE LUFFY.
DOMP DOMP...
HE'S THAT HUGE AND HE'S GOT LUFFY'S FIGHTING SKILLS.
THAT'S DANGEROUS.
LET'S... LET'S JUST GIVE UP ON YOUR SHADOWS.
NO!!!
EVEN IF WE DID, WE STILL HAVE TO SAVE NAMI!! PULL YOURSELF TOGETHER!!
BUT THE PROBLEM IS THAT USOPP AND I ARE DOWN HERE NOW.
...WE CAN'T GET TO THAT MAST MANSION BECAUSE THE BRIDGE IS BROKEN.
RMRMRM...
IT'S TOO FAR FOR US TO JUMP.
EVEN IF WE CHANGE OUR ROUTE AND TAKE THIS PASSAGE...
WE'VE LOST OUR SHORTCUT!
IF WE TAKE A DETOUR WE'LL JUST RUN INTO MORE ZOMBIES.

WAIT 30 SECONDS MORE. I DON'T LIKE THE LOOK OF THIS RAILING.
DOOM
KLANGA
IT'S A BRIDGE!!!
I HAD MORE THAN ENOUGH MATERIAL WITH ALL THIS DEBRIS AND WOOD.
TMP TMP TMP
WHAT? YOU WANT ME TO DO A HALF-BAKED CONSTRUCTION JOB?!
FOR A MAKESHIFT BRIDGE, YOU PUT WAY TOO MUCH EFFORT INTO THE DETAILS.
NAH, YOU'RE A GREAT HELP! BUT ANYWAY, LET'S GO!

RM RM
TMP TMP TMP...
RM RM...

WHAT'S THIS ROOM?
SEEMS WAY TOO DECORATED FOR ITS OWN GOOD.

DOOM!
HORO HORO HORO!
!
I WAS GOING TO HAVE THE ZOMBIES GET YOU AT THE STAIRS BY THE BRIDGE...
...BUT I NEVER EXPECTED OARS TO FALL THROUGH...
HE CAN BE SO CUMBERSOME!
THOSE GHOSTS... YOU'RE THE ONE CONTROLLING THEM?
WHAT ARE THESE THINGS?!
HORO HORO HORO!
NEGATIVE
NEGATIVE!
YOU ALL KNOW ALREADY...
...HOW FEARSOME THESE GHOSTS CAN BE.

I CAN CREATE SPIRITS EASILY USING THE POWERS OF THE HOLLOW-HOLLOW FRUIT!
FLIIIM
HORO HORO HORO! AND NOW YOU MEET YOUR END!!!
THESE GHOSTS ARE A PART OF ME, AND THEY CAN EMPTY HUMAN HEARTS!!
HAH!!
?!!
WHOA. THIS LITTLE CUTIE...
...IS THE MASTERMIND BEHIND ALL THOSE IRRITATING GHOSTS?!
THERE'S NO TIME FOR THAT! IF WE GET HIT BY THOSE THINGS, IT'S OVER!
WE GOTTA RUN!
YOU'RE RIGHT ABOUT THAT!!
NEGATIVE HOLLOW !!
!!!!
AAAH ...

IT'S OVER...
I KNOW! I WISH SOME STRAY DOG WOULD STOMP ON ME!
I'M DUMBER THAN A MACKEREL! I SHOULD JUST DIE.
I APOLOGIZE FOR EVEN STANDING ON THE SAME GROUND AS YOU GUYS...
CAPTURE THEM!!!
GLOOM...
PLOP
SOB...
THRUM
YES, MA'AM!
RAAAA
YEAH !!
THIS WAS TOO EASY. THE ONLY ONES LEFT ARE THOSE ON THE UPPER FLOOR.
GATLING SALT STAR!!!
?!!
GULP!
GULP!
WHO IS THAT?!
AAAH!
...
SSKK...
FLOP... FLOP...!!
?!!

YOU'RE NOT GONNA LAY A FINGER...
...ON MY CREW!!!
HE ONLY PRETENDED TO BE HIT BY THE GHOSTS!
NEGATIVE HOLLOW!!!
MY NAME IS...
?!
...CAPTAIN USOPP!!
WHY? WHY DON'T YOU FALL TO YOUR KNEES?!
I SAW MY GHOST ATTACK YOU! HOW DID YOU DEFEND YOURSELF?!
I DIDN'T!!!

DOOM
I'M ALREADY ...
...EX-TREMELY NEGATIVE !!!!
YOWSA...?!!!
WHAAAAT ?!!

...
...!!
IT CAN'T BE! NO HUMAN IS IMMUNE TO THE NEGATIVE HOLLOWS!
PLOP...!!
HE SURVIVED THE NEGATIVE POWER OF THE GHOSTS!
BUZZ BUZZ!!
HE'S UNDEFEATABLE!!
HUMANS ARE SUPPOSED TO BE POSITIVE...
...AS LONG AS THEY'RE ALIVE! BUT THIS GUY...!!!!
PLIP...
CHEER UP!!!
YEEAAAH...
DON'T TRY TO CHEER ME UP!!!
GET UP, GUYS!
HURRY AND SAVE NAMI AND BROOK!!!
GASP
YOU GUYS... YOU DON'T STAND A CHANCE AGAINST HER IN THAT STATE!!

I'LL TAKE CARE OF THIS!!!
CURSE YOU!!
WHY DOES HE SEEM SO STEADY?
THE NEGATIVE THOUGHTS DIDN'T WORK ON HIM?
...
TAKE CARE OF THE ZOMBIES AROUND HERE BEFORE YOU GO!!
I CAN'T BEAT THEM!
I'D JUST DIE!
I'LL LEAVE THIS ENTIRE PLACE TO YOU!!
HEY, WAIT! DON'T GO YET!
THRILLER BARK, CHURCH
OOO...
ABSALOM...
...DO YOU PROMISE TO TAKE NAMI...
...AS YOUR WIFE, AND TO CHERISH HER FOREVER...
...IN SICKNESS AND IN HEALTH?
RAH
RAH
RAH
YEAH! I DO!!
KLAP KLAP
WOO-HOO!!
KLAP KLAP
BUZZ BUZZ

AND NAMI...
DO YOU PROMISE TO TAKE ABSALOM AS YOUR HUSBAND...
RAH
RAH
...AND LOVE HIM FOREVER?
RAH
YES. I ROTTEN DO.
I LOVE YOU, AB! ♡
SKWIK SKWIK
RAAAH
YEAH!!
YOU MAY NOW KISS THE BRIDE.
YES.
THMP THMP
KISS!
RAH!
RAH!
RAH!

Q: I have a question for you Oda Sensei-chapaa! Is Captain T-Bone a Zombie General? He's all bones, so maybe he's a relative of Brook's?

--Resident of Chapapa Village

A: That's a good question. He's not a Wild Zombie and he's not a Surprise Zombie. Zombie Soldiers don't carry weapons, so by the process of elimination, Captain T-Bone is, as you say, a Zombie General since he's armed. (Note: He's really human)

Q: Horo horo horo! **Negative Hollow!!** FLIIT… Oda Sensei! You're getting way too depressed! If you were to be reborn, what would you like to come back as?

--Koby's Classmate

A: I can't do it. I don't think I can go on. I wanna die. If... If I were to be reborn... Let's see, something... I want to be a stain. I want to be a stain on the carpet. And I want to be a really deep stain.

Q: Oda Sensei, I know you must be busy, but I have a question. In volume 46, Nami's pants are a different color in chapter 446 than in chapter 445. Did something happen? *Thriller Bark* is full of mysterious phenomena.

--Makigon

445

446

A: I can't do it. I don't think I can go on. I wanna die. Maybe those pants were made of fabric that faded easily. No, I'm sorry I tried to make excuses. If I were to be reborn, I want to be drool, and drool all over the place.

Chapter 462: ADVENTURES OF OARS

ENERU'S GREAT SPACE MISSION, VOL. 28:
"ATTACK NOW, ASK QUESTIONS LATER"

NEGATIVE HOLLOW !!!
HORO HORO HORO!
!!!
THAT MUST HAVE BEEN SOME KIND OF FLUKE! AFTER THAT FULL FIRE ATTACK...
...NO DOUBT YOU'VE NOW LOST ALL OF YOUR WILL TO LIVE!!!
...
HE TOOK THE HIT! ALL FOUR OF THEM!
HORO HORO HORO!
NEGATIVE♪ NEGATIVE♪ NEGATIVE♪
SINCE THE BEGINNING OF THRILLER BARK...
...NOT ONE PERSON HAS ESCAPED THE EFFECTS OF...

?!!
WHOA !!!
DOOM
GLOOOM
THE NEGATIVE GHOSTS WERE OUT-NEGATIVED !!!
RM RM RM...
COULD HE BE SOME KIND OF SAGE--OR A SAINT?!!
I'M SO SORRY FOR EVERYTHING, KUMACY.
IT'S EVEN AFFECTING MISTRESS PERONA!!!
GLOOM
LISTEN, ALL OF YOU.
WHEN IT COMES TO THINKING ABOUT THINGS PESSIMISTICALLY...
RM RM RM RM...
...!!
...NO ONE CAN BEAT ME!!!!
BAM
HE'S SO CONFIDENT ABOUT HIS TERRIBLE CHARACTER TRAIT!!!
HUH?!!

PERONA'S WONDER GARDEN
RMRMRMRMRM...
HUFF
HUFF
I NEVER THOUGHT USOPP'S PESSIMISM WOULD COME IN HANDY HERE.
IF IT WEREN'T FOR HIM...
...THE ENTIRE CREW MIGHT'VE BEEN DONE FOR!!
THOSE ARE SOME REALLY AWFUL POWERS.
ONLY THE STRANGE ANIMAL ZOMBIES ARE COMING AFTER US.
THE MANSION BROOK WENT TO IS STRAIGHT AHEAD FROM THIS GARDEN.
I'M TAKING OFF FROM HERE TO FIND NAMI!
ALL RIGHT. GOOD LUCK, MAN!
YEAH! I'M A BURNING BALL OF LOVE!!
NAMI! I WON'T LET YOU GET MARRIED!!!
BOUF!!
HE FLEW? AREN'T WE PRETTY HIGH UP?!

PEOPLE SAY YOU DON'T FEEL PAIN WHEN THE ADRENALINE'S PUMPING.
KRASH!!
ANYWAY, WE'RE GOING TO HEAD UP TO THE TOP FLOOR OF THAT MANSION.
WOOD
THE SKELETON IS IN THE LABORATORY!
GOT IT.
KLANK!!
K LANK!!
SWAK!!
DOOM!!
YO HO HO HO.
KRAKK!!
OOF!
HUFF...!!
HUFF
HUFF

YOU'RE LIKE A PHOENIX... WELL, MORE LIKE A ZOMBIE.
YOU SHOULDN'T BE ABLE TO STAND UP ANYMORE.
HEEZ
HEEZ
I'M GOING TO TAKE YOU DOWN FOR GOOD...
...SO YOU CAN NEVER COME BACK TO RETAKE YOUR SHADOW.
WHICH PART SHALL I CUT OFF USING MY SPECIAL NOTCH SLASH?
...!!
YOU DON'T KNOW ANYTHING ABOUT THAT MOVE...
HEEZ
...SO DON'T USE THAT NAME.
HEEZ
I USED TO SERVE IN MY KINGDOM'S RAIDER SQUAD. THE QUICK DRAW ATTACK AT WHICH I WAS MOST SKILLED WAS...
...REQUIEM LEBANDEROLE. MY COMRADES-IN-ARMS RENAMED IT WITH REGARD TO MY SWORD FIGHTING TECHNIQUE.
?
THREE-PACE HUM NOTCH SLASH.

YOU MAY HAVE MY PERSONALITY AND SKILLS...
...BUT YOU'VE FORGOTTEN ALL THE MEMORIES AND HUMANITY!
YOU HAVE NO RIGHT TO USE THAT NAME!!!
...
YO HO HO HO. IF YOU INSIST ON BEING THE ORIGINAL...
...THEN TRY TO DEFEAT ME, THE **FAKE**, WITH YOUR SWORD.
THIS...
...IS YOUR LAST CHANCE.
CHNK!
...!!
HUFF...
HUFF...
HUFF...
WOBL...
SWP...
HUFF...
THUMP...
HUFF...
THUMP...

THUMP...
THUMP...
THUMP...
THUMP...
KLEK
KLAK...
THREE-PACE HUM...
TMP...
TMP...
DO OM!!
...NOTCH SLASH !!
!!!

FLOP...
LABOON
...
KLANK
..!!
FIFTY YEARS IN THESE DARK WATERS! IT WAS SO LONG, AND IT WAS ALL FOR NOTHING!
I'LL START WITH THE AFRO.
I WANT TO APOLOGIZE FOR MY UNFORTUNATE END!!
SHKK...
...I WANT TO APOLOGIZE TO YOU MORE THAN ANYTHING!!
YO HO HO.
VING...!!
MY LIFE WAS SO DREARY !!!
SO DESOLATE !!!

BOOM!!
?!!
HUH?!
KRMB
KRMB...
HEY! WHAT'S THIS RUMBLING?!
I DON'T KNOW! MAYBE IT'S AN EARTHQUAKE!!
HUFF
HUFF
TMP TMP TMP...
WHAT IS THIS?! THE BUILDING IS SHAKING!
HM?!
SHK
RMRMRM...
AAAH!
WUP WUP
RMRMRMRMRM
HUH...?
THERE HE IS!! HEY, SKELETON!!!
IS THIS THE LAB?!
BAM!!
HUFF
HUFF

YOU SEEM PRETTY BEAT UP...
...BUT YOU'RE STILL ALIVE!! YOU'RE ALIVE, RIGHT?
W-WHAT ARE YOU DOING HERE?
...
YO HO HO! NO TOUCHING THE LOSER WITHOUT MY PERMISSION!!
!
KLANG
HOLD IT RIGHT THERE.
CHAK!!
?!!!

SO YOU'RE...
...THAT LEGENDARY SAMURAI WHO SLEW A DRAGON IN ANCIENT TIMES.
I DON'T EVEN KNOW IF I BELIEVE DRAGONS REALLY EXISTED, BUT...
...
SHING!!
CLANK
!!!
...I'VE WANTED TO MEET YOU!
SKRINK..!!!
SHKK..!!
HE'S AN AGGRESSIVE, THREE-SWORD-WIELDING PIRATE SWORDSMAN.
HE'S PRETTY STRONG. IF YOUR PRIDE WON'T GET IN THE WAY...
...HE COULD TAKE YOUR PLACE AND FIGHT TO GET YOUR SHADOW BACK. WHAT DO YOU SAY?
WHOA...
YOU'RE REALLY SHAKING!!
RM RM RM RM RM...
MY SHADOW?! REALLY? PLEASE!
...
RM RM
HE...PUSHED HIM AWAY...
WHO *IS* THIS GUY?!

PLEASE!! PLEASE!! PLEASE GET BACK MY SHADO...
GAH!!
SHUT IT!!!
HUH?!
OOPS.
HEY, SKELETON !!
THAT SWORD... IT LOOKS NICE.
YO HO HO! YOU HAVE A GOOD EYE.
RM RM
RM RM
THE SHUSUI BLADE IS A LEGENDARY SWORD.
THIS IS INDEED ONE OF THE 21 EX-CELLENT GRADE SWORDS. BLACK BLADE WITH A REVERSE WAVED TEMPER LINE!
YOU DON'T GET TO ENCOUNTER IT JUST ANY DAY.
AN EXCELLENT GRADE SWORD! THAT'S GREAT.
RM RM RM
I HEARD YOU WERE A SAMURAI, SO I WAS HOPING YOU HAD A GOOD SWORD.
ALL RIGHT THEN...
I'LL MAKE THAT SWORD MINE!!
GRIN...
WHAT ?!

MAST MANSION, FIRST FLOOR CHURCH
AAAH!
RM RM RM RM RM
AAAH!
SHK SHK!!
SMOOCH!
SMOOCH!
SMOOCH!
HEY!! STOP IT! WHAT'S WITH ALL THE SHAKING?!!
GROWR!!
I CAN'T EVEN KISS MY BRIDE!!!
SIR ABSALOM!!
SKRUNK!
CHAK!
WHAT?! DID YOU FIND OUT WHAT'S CAUSING THIS?!
OUR SHIP, THRILLER BARK, IS CAUGHT IN A GIANT SEA CURRENT!!!
THE WHOLE ISLAND IS SHAKING!!

DOOM!!
HOW DID THAT HAPPEN?!
IT'S THAT SPECIAL ZOMBIE! HE'S RANDOMLY STEERING THE SHIP!!
HEY, IT MOVED.
TUGG TUGG...
WHAT?!
RMRMRM RM RM...
ZOMBIE GENERALS, GO! ALL OF YOU!
KREEK...
RMRMRM
STOP OARS!
YES, SIR!!
KLANK!!
HUH?
KLANK!!
!
STOP IT RIGHT THERE, SPECIAL ZOMBIE OARS!!

CHOP HIM DOWN FROM THE FEET!!!
YEAH!!
... GATLING !!!!
HUH ...?!
POOF!!!
HE DISAPPEARED! WHERE DID OARS GO?!
HE'S SO BIG...
SWV-SWV
...HOW CAN HE BE THAT QUICK?!
AAAAH!!!
GUM-GUM... (EVEN THOUGH I'M NOT MADE OF RUBBER)...
THERE HE IS! LOOK UP!!
?!!

?!!
BOOM BOOM BO

KRMF
KRMF!!
DON'T GET IN THE WAY...
...OF MY ADVENTURE!!!
GRAAAA
AAAAAH!!
THEY'VE BEEN ANNIHILATED?!
ALL THOSE WHO WERE JUST HERE?!
Y-YES! THEY'RE ALL FLATTENED!!
THEY'RE OUR STRONGEST ARMY OF ZOMBIES! THEY'RE THE ZOMBIE GENERALS!!
YES. IT HAPPENED IN AN INSTANT!!!
IT CAN'T BE...

ISN'T OARS SUPPOSED TO BE ON OUR SIDE?!
WHY IS HE CAUSING SO MUCH TROUBLE?!
TMP TMP TMP TMP T
OVER THERE, RIGHT?!
SHKKK...!!
YES! NOW LET ME GO, PLEASE!!
ZOMBIES ARE ONLY SUPPOSED TO KNOW HOW TO OBEY!! IF WE LET THAT THING RUN FREE...
...WHAT WILL HAPPEN TO THRILLER BARK?!
BANG!!
NAMIIII !!!
I'M HERE FOR YOOOOU!!!
?!!
DOOM!!
THERE YOU ARE!!!
YOU'RE ONE OF THE STRAW HAT PIRATES?!!

Q: Hey, Odacchi. I love your comics. So I have a question for you. What happens when Chopper eats four Rumble Balls? I've always wondered about that. Please illustrate what will happen.

--Hama-chan

A: Sure. After → three of them, the powers of the Devil Fruit will go out of control... After the fourth one, the author loses control.

IT'S MY TREAT!

HIS TRADEMARK PHRASE.

Q: Hello, Oda Sensei! This is the first letter I've ever sent you! On page 161 of volume 46, in the chapter titled "Moria," there's a zombie numbered "767." But on page 173, in the chapter titled "The Four Monsters of Thriller Bark," there's a zombie numbered "741." Why is that? Is it…a mistake?! Please answer me!

--Snow Drop Growing in Drum Kingdom

741
THAT PROVES IT.
HE SAID THAT IT'S ALMOST COMPLETE.

A: You really took an in-depth look. So you're saying that it doesn't make sense for higher numbered zombies to be made after lower numbered zombies, right?! But it's actually fine the way it is. Zombies get purified all the time and those numbers go missing. Either something happened to the original owner of the shadow or the zombie got purified by an intruder. Moria thinks of the zombies as simply expendable soldiers, so they just reuse a zombie's number once it goes away. That's why there are some zombies with lower numbers that are created at later dates. By the way, you might not care about this, but there is a rule to how the zombies are numbered. Wild Zombie: 0-199, Surprise Zombie: 200-399, Soldier Zombie: 400-199, Zombie General: 800-899, Special Zombie: 900. When any of the numbers go missing, new zombies are made to fill in.

Chapter 463:
PIRATE SANJI VS. MYSTERY MAN ABSALOM

ENERU'S GREAT SPACE MISSION, VOL. 29:
"SPACE PIRATE EXCAVATION PROJECT"

WHAT'S GOING ON?
RM RM
RM...
THERE'S WAY TOO MUCH SHAKING.
THE SHIP PROBABLY JUST CAUGHT SOME BAD CURRENTS.
RM RM RM...
IT'S *PROBABLY* YOUR FAULT. KI SHI SHI!
SO WHAT DO YOU WANT? WHY ARE YOU HERE?
...
OH YEAH! YOU STOLE MY SHADOW FROM ME!!
YOU'RE GOING TO GIVE IT BACK! AND ZOLO'S AND SANJI'S...
...AND BROOK'S AND THAT OLD MAN ZOMBIE'S TOO! ALL OF THEM!!
WELL, AREN'T YOU GREEDY? HOW DO YOU THINK YOU'RE GOING TO ACCOMPLISH THAT?

I JUST HAVE TO BEAT YOU UP, RIGHT?
EVEN IF YOU BEAT ME OR KILL ME...
...THE ZOMBIES WILL SIMPLY LOSE THEIR MASTER. THE SHADOWS STAY WHERE THEY ARE.
MY POWERS CONTROL THE SHADOWS. TO GET WHAT YOU WANT...
...YOU'LL HAVE TO MAKE ME TELL THE SHADOWS, "GO BACK TO YOUR ORIGINAL OWNERS"...
...SINCE I'M THEIR CURRENT MASTER.
SO IF YOU DO THAT, ALL THE SHADOWS WILL RETURN?
KI SHI SHI. THAT'S RIGHT. ISN'T IT SIMPLE?
YOU MIGHT EVEN BE ABLE TO MAKE ME DO IT IF YOU COULD MAKE ME WEAK ENOUGH.
BUT YOU CAN'T TOUCH ME.
YAWN!
WIP WIP
ALL RIGHT. **GUM-GUM...**

SMA
...PISTOL !!!
SH
!
A SHADOW?!
SSKK...
KI SHI SHI. GO AHEAD AND TRY...
...TO WIN AGAINST MY DOUBLE...
SSKK...
...THE DOPPELMAN !!
SSKK

ZWOOM...!!!
WHOA!
IN THE PAST I TOO, WAS FULL OF AMBITION AND OVERCONFIDENT IN MY OWN ABILITIES.
WHAT IS THAT THING? GET IT OUT OF THE WAY!!
BUT THEN I REALIZED HOW IMPORTANT IT WAS TO HAVE SUPERIOR UNDERLINGS.
I WILL NEVER DO ANYTHING ON MY OWN AGAIN. I'LL BECOME THE PIRATE KING BY SIMPLY USING THE HELP OF OTHERS.
I'M THE ONE WHO'S GONNA BE THE PIRATE KING!!!
YOUR ZOMBIE SAID THE SAME EXACT THING.
WHEN THERE IS AN EXTREME SIZE DIFFERENCE BETWEEN THE SHADOW AND THE BODY...
...THE CHARACTER OF THE SHADOW'S ORIGINAL OWNER LINGERS ON.
WHOA!
KRASH!!
KRASH!
BUT IT'S ONLY A MATTER OF TIME.

SOONER OR LATER, ALL YOUR MEMORIES WILL BE LOST...
...AND THE ZOMBIE WILL BECOME COMPLETELY OBEDIENT TO ME.
GRR
NO MATTER HOW STRONG ITS WILL MAY BE...
...EVERY ZOMBIE EVENTUALLY BECOMES COMPLETELY OBEDIENT.
I'LL GET IT BACK RIGHT AWAY, THEN!!!
KRAK...!!
?!
GUM-GUM...
...GATLING !!!
UWIP UWIP!!
BRICK BAT!!!
POP POP OP OP!!
WOOO...!!!

!!
KR AK!!!
BAM!!
BAM BAM
BAM
BAM BAM BAM!!!
HMMHM... ♪
ALL MY PUNCHES ARE GETTING BLOCKED!!
I CAN'T HIT HIM!!!
FLUP!!
CHOMP!!
AHH!
OW!!!

KI SHI SHI! DON'T WORRY, THEY'RE NOT GOING TO SUCK YOUR BLOOD.
OWWW!!!
YOU'RE GOING TO BEAT ME UP? DON'T MAKE ME LAUGH!
AUGH!!!
WAM!!
GET AWAY!!!
SMAK!!
SHLUK...
WHEN AN INEXPERIENCED YOUTH MISJUDGES THE SITUATION...
RMRMRMRM...
SSKK...
...HE SETS HIMSELF UP FOR MASSIVE HUMILIATION.
HUFF
GRR! NOW I'M MAD!!!
HUFF

HUFF
HUFF
TUMP!
GUM-GUM...
WHAT NOW? HE JUMPED OFF THE EDGE...
TRYING TO RUN AWAY?
?!!
... STAMP !!!
BAM
OW! YOU LITTLE BRAT!!!
SEE?! SERVES YOU RIGHT! AND YOU THOUGHT I COULDN'T TOUCH YOU!!!

RM RM RM RM
RM RM RM RM RM RM RM RM...
ZWIP!!
HUH?!
WOO!!
LET GO...
JIGG♪
HUH?
JIGG♪
JIGG♪

...OF NAMI, YOU IDIOT!!!
!!!
SHWUUUK...
YOUR KNIGHT IS AT YOUR SERVICE.
FW UP...
I'M HERE, NAMI.
FWOO
KRMB...
DRUP...
PHEW! THAT SURPRISED ME! IT'S NAMI. OKAY, IT'S NAMI...
THUMP THUMP THUMP
HER BEAUTY KNOWS NO BOUNDS!! I ALMOST THOUGHT I HAD SAVED A GODDESS BY MISTAKE!!
WHAT?! A GODDESS?!
...
!!!

WHAT ARE YOU TALKING ABOUT? YOU'RE PART OF THE CREW...
...FROM THAT PIRATE SHIP.
SWUP...!
!
?!!
WHAT?! AN ANGEL?!
OH! NO, SHE'S HUMAN... PHEW, THAT SCARED ME FOR A MINUTE!
I UNDERSTAND. I TOTALLY UNDERSTAND.
THE ONLY THINGS THAT LOOK GOOD IN WHITE ARE NAMI AND RICE.
WHAT ARE THOSE TWO DOING?!
AMEN, BROTHER.
HOOO
WAIT! I HAVE NO INTENTION OF GETTING FRIENDLY WITH YOU, PIRATE!!!
SWOO!!
GIVE ME BACK THE BRIDE!!!
BOOM!!
!!!

!!
RM..RM..RM...
HEY, YOU ALMOST HIT NAMI. YOU SHOULDN'T LAUNCH RECKLESS ATTACKS...
...WHEN THERE'S A LADY AROUND.
DO
OM
I'M SURPRISED YOU DODGED IT.
...
IT SEEMS YOUR SHADOW IS ALREADY GONE.
COME TO THINK OF IT, THERE IS A NEW ZOMBIE WHO'S FIXATED ON THAT WOMAN.
HIS INDIVIDUAL WILL STILL REMAINED, AND HE WASN'T YET COMPLETELY OBEDIENT...
THAT WAS PROBABLY *YOUR* ZOMBIE.
...
SEEING HOW YOUR SHADOW WASN'T EVEN WORTH BEING PLACED IN A ZOMBIE GENERAL'S BODY...
...YOUR BATTLE SKILLS ARE PROBABLY MINIMAL.
IN FACT, THAT PENGUIN WAS ALL BARK AND NO BITE.

I'M ONE OF THE **MYSTERIOUS FOUR** AND I COMMAND ALL OF THE ZOMBIE GENERALS.
YOU THINK YOU STAND A CHANCE AGAINST ME?!
THUMP
THUMP
HUPP!
WHOA! I THOUGHT I JUST SAW AN ANGEL!
I'M WARNING YOU...
LEAVE THAT WOMAN HERE AND GO BACK TO LIVING IN THE SHADOWS.
I'M BUSY RIGHT NOW. MY MOST POWERFUL UNDERLINGS...
...SEEM TO HAVE BEEN CRUSHED BY YOUR CAPTAIN'S ZOMBIE.
I NEED TO KISS THE BRIDE BEFORE I GO AND TAKE CARE OF IT.
DO YOU UNDERSTAND? I'M REALLY ANNOYED RIGHT NOW!
GROWRRR
I DON'T HAVE TIME TO DEAL WITH WEAKLINGS LIKE...
...YOU!

SHUT YOUR MOUTH, YOU BEAST-FACED WEDDING GUY!!!
AWHAA ?!!
SIR ABSALOM !!!
NO WAY! HE WEIGHS OVER 600 POUNDS AND GOT KNOCKED BACK JUST LIKE THAT?!
FWIK...
THAT INVISIBLE MAN USOPP WAS TALKING ABOUT...
...MUST BE YOU.
TMP..
...?!!

WHAT'S WITH HIS KICKS?! HOGBACK TRANSPLANTED THE POWER OF THE WILDERNESS INTO THIS BODY. THERE'S NO WAY HE SHOULD BE ABLE TO KNOCK ME BACK LIKE THIS...
HANDS OF THE DEAD!!!
SWUP!!
BOOM!!
SKREK!
SKREK!
BOOM!
?!!
WHAT?! HOW DID YOU KNOW WHAT I WAS GOING TO DO?!
BASSES CÔTE BLAST!!
GAH!!
THWAK!!

LONGE LASHER!!
TENDRON TENDER-IZER!!
BAM!!
BAM!
WHOA!!
OOF!
YOU'RE THE INVISIBLE BEAST WHO LICKED ROBIN BACK ON SUNNY, AREN'T YOU?!
FLANCHET FLAYER!!
QUASI CRACKER!! QUEUE CRIPPLER!! CUISSEAU CRUSHER!!
YOU'RE ALSO THE ONE WHO PEEPED ON NAMI TAKING A BATH, AREN'T YOU?!!
GAH!!
WAK!
BWAK!!
WHAT IS THIS POWER?! CAN THIS BE THE POWER OF A PETTY PIRATE UNDERLING?!
SMAK!!
...!!
WHY IS SHE UNCONSCIOUS RIGHT NOW?!
YOU BETTER NOT HAVE DONE ANYTHING NASTY AROUND HER!!
JARRET JARRER!!
YOU WANT TO MARRY HER? SAY IT TO MY FACE! I'LL PULVERIZE YOU AND TURN YOU INTO A CROQUETTE!!!
AIGH!
KRAKRAK-!!!
WHACK!!!

I'M GOING TO GO INTO HIDING FOR NOW!!
INVISI-SKATING!!
VIIIP...
!
USOPP'S SPECIAL...
...SALT BALL!
POP!
FLIP FLIP FLIP...!!
!!
VE
EN
THERE YOU ARE.
KRMB
KRMB...
AGH! WHAT IS THIS?! IT TASTES SO SALTY!
VEAU VENGEANCE!!
WOOAH!!!

KAKRASH!!!
!!!
...!!
THIS IS IMPOSSIBLE! HE DOESN'T EVEN HAVE A BOUNTY ON HIS HEAD!!!
EARLIER YOU SAID YOU WERE "ANNOYED"...
WHAT I'M FEELING RIGHT NOW DOESN'T EVEN COMPARE!!!
...
KRMB...
RM RM RM RM RM RM RM...
I'M SO ANGRY I'M ABOUT TO EXPLODE!!!
HE DID!!
BWOOF!!
OOOOOO
...!!
HUFF HUFF...
AND UNFORTUNATELY FOR YOU...
...THERE'S SOMETHING ELSE ABOUT YOU THAT'S MAKING ME MAD.
WOOO
?!!

Chapter 464: SANJI'S DREAM

WAN
฿667,00
Tenth

...
KRMBL...
...!!
HUFF
UGH...!
HUFF
SIR ABSALOM!
HUFF... YOU'RE HOLDING A GRUDGE AGAINST ME?!
THAT'S RIGHT.
YOU'VE...
...STOLEN ONE OF MY DREAMS.
?!

KRMB...
GROWR! I HAVE NO RECOLLECTION OF THAT.
MAYBE YOU'RE MISTAKEN.
THIS IS THE FIRST TIME I'VE EVER MET YOU!
HUFF... HUFF...!!
I'LL BLOW YOU AWAY...
...WITH MY HANDS OF THE DEAD!!
SWOO...!!
TAKE THEM OFF!!!
!
I SAID, TAKE THOSE BAZOOKAS OFF YOUR ARMS.
WHAT?!
YOU DON'T GET IT? IF YOU HURT NAMI WITH THOSE EXPLOSIONS OF YOURS...
...I'LL BEAT YOU TO AN UNRECOGNIZ-ABLE PULP.

HMPH! THERE'S NO WAY HE CAN KNOW!!
BOOM!!
VIP!!
!!
I TOLD YOU TO...
!!
KR AK!!!
...TAKE THEM OFF!!!
BA-BASH!!
?!!
TUNK!!

WHAT?! WHERE DID THOSE BAZOOKAS COME FROM?!
I KNEW IT WAS SOME-THING LIKE THAT.
THAT'S THE KIND OF ATTACK YOU WOULD COME UP WITH.
DOOM!!
...!!
YOU CAN MAKE YOURSELF INVISIBLE, ALONG WITH...
...ANYTHING YOU TOUCH.
THAT'S YOUR POWER!
THE INVISIBLE MAN OF THE CLEAR-CLEAR FRUIT.
I KNOW ABOUT EVERY-THING...
...THAT YOU CAN DO!!
?!
WHAT ARE YOU?!
WHO ARE YOU?!

DID THAT GUY MEET SIR ABSALOM SOMEWHERE BEFORE?!
WHY'S HE HOLDING A GRUDGE AGAINST HIM?!
WHEN I WAS A KID, I READ THROUGH THE ENCYCLOPEDIA OF DEVIL FRUITS.
I WASN'T THAT INTERESTED IN THEM, SINCE THEY DIDN'T SEEM REAL AND EACH POWER COMES WITH A CURSE.
BUT THERE WAS ONE ENTRY THAT STRUCK AWE IN MY HEART.
IF I WERE ABLE, SOMETIME IN MY LIFE, TO GAIN THIS POWER...
...EVEN IF IT CURSED ME, I'D STILL WANT TO EAT THAT FRUIT.
BUT THERE ARE NO TWO OF THE SAME FRUIT IN THIS WORLD.
?
SO IF I MET SOMEONE WITH THAT POWER, I'D KNOW MY DREAM WAS OVER!
DO YOU UNDERSTAND?! THERE WAS A TIME WHEN I WANTED TO BECOME AN INVISIBLE MAN!!!
AND NOW YOU'VE RUINED MY DREAM OF EATING THE CLEAR-CLEAR FRUIT!
!!
HIS ANGER IS TOTALLY MISPLACED!!

OH, HOW I DREAMED OF IT!!
IF I HAD THAT POWER, I'D GO TO THE WOMEN'S CHANGING ROOM AND... NO! I MEAN, I THOUGHT ABOUT HOW MUCH GOOD I COULD DO WITH IT...
I'D GO TO THE WOMEN'S BATHS AND... I MEAN, I COULD SAVE SO MANY LIVES WITH A POWER LIKE THAT!!
HIS HEAD IS FULL OF DREAMS ABOUT PEEPING ON WOMEN!!!
OOOOO!!!
SHUT UP! THANKS TO MY YEARS OF DAYDREAMS AND FANTASIES...
...I UNDERSTAND EVERYTHING THAT COULD BE ACCOMPLISHED WITH THIS POWER!!!
ADDING THAT TO HOW MUCH DANGER YOU PUT NAMI IN...
...I'LL MAKE YOU PAY FOR IT ALL! YOU BETTER BE PREPARED TO DIE!!!
BWOOF!!
...!!
I WAS WONDERING WHAT THIS WAS ABOUT... IT'S JUST SOME STUPID GRUDGE!!
YOU'RE BEING ABSURD!!!
YOU PERVERT!!!
?!!

LIKE YOU'RE ONE TO TALK!
SMAKA
YOU'RE ABSOLUTELY RIGHT!!!
GAH!!!
YOU'RE BOTH EQUALLY BAD!!
HUH?!!
KRASH!!!
FWAP...!!
...!!
I COMPLETELY UNDERSTAND YOUR GRUDGE AND YOUR ANGER, BUT I'LL STILL DEFEAT YOU!!
!

DOOM!
I DON'T JUST HAVE THE HEAD OF A LION!!
I'VE GOT THE SKIN OF AN ELEPHANT AND THE MUSCLES FROM BEARS AND GORILLAS. I WEIGH IN AT OVER 600 POUNDS!!
IT'S ALL DR. HOGBACK'S DOING...
...THROUGH TRANSPLANT AFTER TRANSPLANT, THIS BODY OF MINE IS A MASTERPIECE OF THE POWER OF THE WILD!!!
THE POWER OF THE CLEAR-CLEAR FRUIT IS NOTHING BUT AN ACCESSORY TO MY TRUE STRENGTH!
GROWRR!!!
BUT STILL YOU PEEPED!!!
GWAGH!!!
HE'S RIGHT!!

...!!
KRMBL...
NORMAL PEOPLE WOULD BREAK THEIR LEGS IF THEY TRIED TO KICK ME, YET HE'S KICKING ME LIKE IT'S NOTHING...
BUT I'LL BE THE LAST ONE TO LAUGH!!
VWOOP...
VIP...
IN ADDITION TO HAVING THIS POWER THAT YOU DESIRED...
...I'LL ALSO TAKE THE WOMAN YOU LOVE AS MY BRIDE!!
THAT WILL BE THE BITTERNESS OF YOUR DEFEAT!!!
!
AND THEN NAMI DISAPPEARED TOO, AND WE COULDN'T CHASE AFTER HER ANYMORE!
...!!!
YOU WANT TO MAKE NAMI INVISIBLE TOO?!!
GRAP!!
YOU'RE NOT TAKING HER!!!
GROWRR!!
...
IT'S NO USE. FEEL THE POWER OF THE MYSTERY MAN HANDLER!!

KR
AK!!
!!
HUPP...!!
WOBBLE...
UGH!!!
GROWR, I SEE. SO YOU WANT TO SACRIFICE YOURSELF...
...FOR THE SAKE OF THAT WOMAN?! JUST TRY AND PROTECT HER.
MYSTERY MAN HANDLER !!!
!!!
KRAK!!
MYSTERY MAN KICKER !!!
HA HA HA! YOU BETTER NOT LET GO OF THAT WOMAN!!
SWOOP...
SMAK!!
OOF!!!
BAM!!
BASH
JAB!!!
!!!
BOOM
...!!
SWUP... !!
I'M SORRY, NAMI!!!
FLUMP!!
AH HA HA! YOU LET HER GO!!
SO I GUESS YOU DON'T WANT TO SACRIFICE YOUR LIFE FOR HER AFTER ALL!!!

I'M SORRY... HUFF... I DON'T WANT MY BLOOD...
PLIP...
...TO STAIN YOUR WHITE DRESS.
PLIP...
KOFF...
THAT INVISIBLE MAN IS HIDING LIKE THE COWARD THAT HE IS.
I NO LONGER REGRET LOSING MY DREAM.
HUFF
PLIP...
PLIP...
HUFF
I...
I DON'T CARE ANYMORE IF I CAN'T BE INVISIBLE!!
I'LL GO PEEPING USING MY OWN POWERS.
PLIP...
YOU'RE STILL GOING TO GO PEEPING?!!!
!
SPLAK...
GRAP!!!
?!!
GRRR! LET GO OF ME!!!
HA HA! YOU THINK I'LL LET GO NOW, YOU STUPID IDIOT?
IF YOU'RE ALL THOSE DIFFERENT ANIMALS...
...YOU'D MAKE FOR SOME GOOD GROUND MEAT!!!

SHUT UP! LET GO OF ME!!
BAM!! BAM!!
...!!
SWIP...
VEEN!!!
...!!!
OOOO
?!
EXTRA HACHIS HASH!!

AWAGH
!!!!
SIR ABSALOM !!!
SHWAK
!!!
!!!
KOFF...
HUFF...
THE WOMEN'S BATH... I MEAN...
HUFF...
HUFF...
A BEAST'S BRIDE SHOULD ONLY BE ANOTHER BEAST!!!
...!!

MAST MANSION, PERONA'S ROOM
TMP TMP TMP
WAIIT ...!!!
HE'S STILL COMING AFTER ME!!
HUFF
IF ONLY I COULD TAKE *HIM* OUT, I COULD BEAT THE REST OF THE PIRATES EASILY!!!
TMP TMP TMP
TMP TMP TMP TMP
STUPID NEGATIVE LONG-NOSE!!
IT'S STILL COMING AFTER ME!!
HUFF
IF ONLY I COULD TAKE *IT* OUT, I COULD BEAT THAT HOLLOW GIRL EASILY!!
TMP
TMP TMP TMP TMP TM
STUPID BEAR ZOMBIE!!!
WAIIT !!!
AHHH! GET AWAY FROM ME!!
WAIT, HOLLOW GIRL!!
AHHH! GET AWAY FROM ME!!
KUMACY! HURRY UP AND GET RID OF HIM!
WAIIT !!!

DON'T YOU LAY A FINGER...
GWOO...
...ON MISTRESS PERONA!!!
AARGH !!!
BOING!!
KABOOOM!!
AIIEE !!!
BOOM BOOM BOOM BOOM
YIKES !!
WHOA !!
WHOA !!
WHOAHHH !!!

I NEVER THOUGHT A STUFFED ANIMAL COULD BE THIS QUICK...
...AND POWERFUL!!
HE CAN'T EVEN REACH THE ZIPPER ON HIS BACK!!
RSTL..
TAKE THIS!!
FLAME BALL !!!!
POOF!
?!!
AAAAH!
TMPTMPTMPTMP
BWOOF
HEY! IT WORKED!!
HAHAHA! I GUESS HE'S JUST ANOTHER ZOMBIE AFTER ALL!
POP!
AND TO FINISH IT OFF WITH SOME OIL...
...IT'S THE "DON'T CROSS THIS LINE" TECHNIQUE!!
HAHAHA! STUPID BEAR!!
NEENER NEENER NEENER!!!
PWOOOF!!
OH.
YOU CAN'T COME OVER HERE ANYMORE!!
HA HA HA! NOW I'M INVINCIBLE!!
I OWN THIS PLACE!
I DON'T LIKE BULLYING THE WEAK, BUT...

ANYWAY, WHERE'S THAT HOLLOW GIRL?
I'M GOING TO HAVE TO PUNISH HER. WHERE'D SHE GO?
OVER HERE, LONG-NOSE!
!
HUH? OUT THE WINDOW? NAH, NO WAY...
THIS FLOOR IS REALLY HIGH UP.
?!!
HUH ?!!
DOOM!!
I'M THE GHOST PRINCESS, IDIOT!
AND I JUST FIGURED OUT HOW TO BEAT YOU! ONCE I TAKE YOU OUT, THE REST OF YOUR CREW IS NOTHING!!
WAIT! SOMETHING'S GONE WRONG!!!
W-WHAT?! WHY ARE YOU FLYING?! I THOUGHT ALL YOU COULD DO WAS MANIPULATE GHOSTS!!!
FLIT FLIT
WHAT EXACTLY IS YOUR POWER?!
HORO HORO HORO...

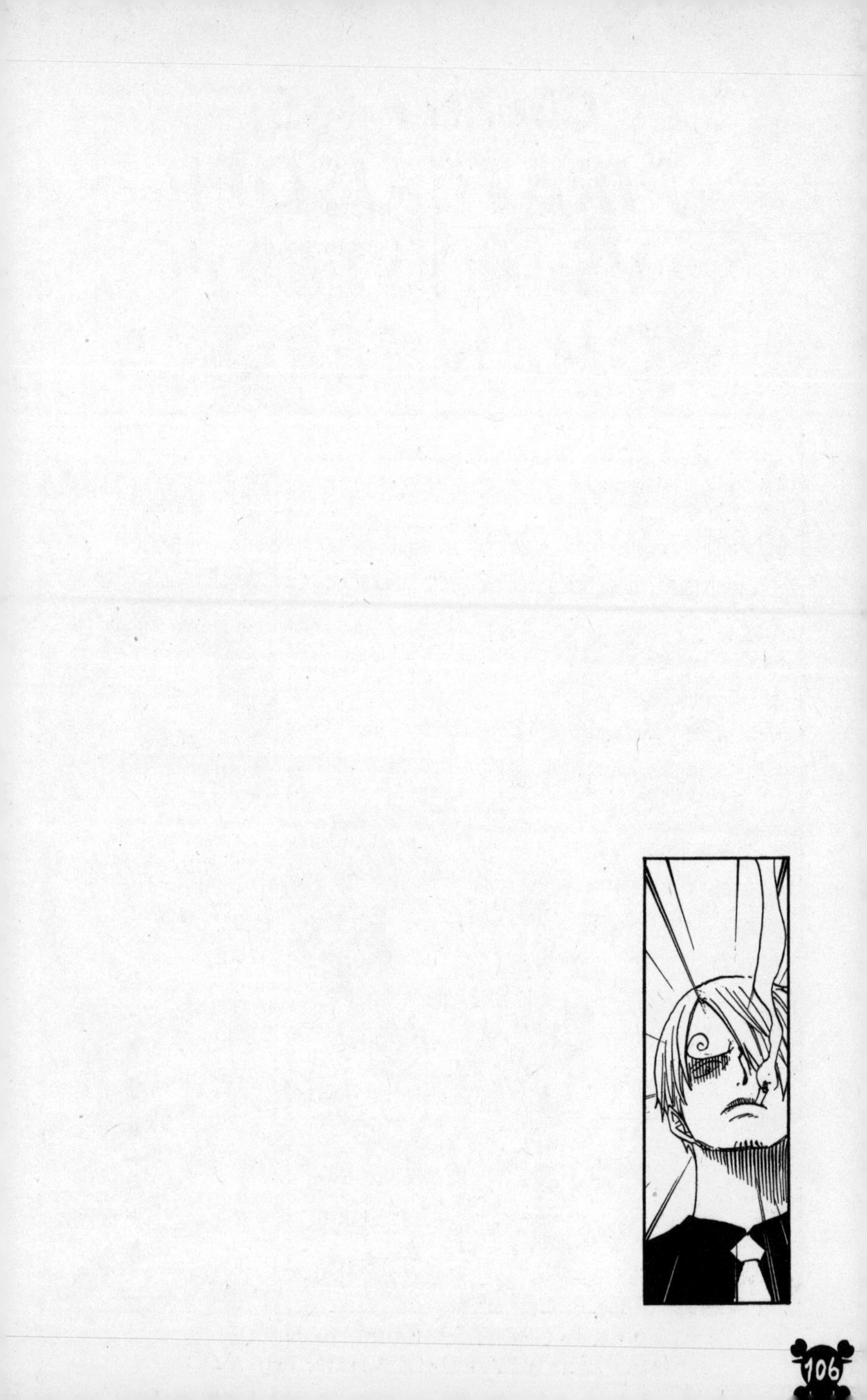

Chapter 465:
PIRATE USOPP VS. MYSTERY WOMAN PERONA

ENERU'S GREAT SPACE MISSION, VOL. 30:
"WHAT LIES BELOWGROUND ON THE MOON"

HOW CAN YOU BE FLYING LIKE THAT?!
HORO HORO HORO!!
I JUST GOT A LITTLE NERVOUS BACK THERE.
I NEVER THOUGHT I WOULD MEET SOMEONE WHO'S IMMUNE TO MY NEGATIVE GHOSTS.
YOU WERE RUNNING SCARED JUST A FEW MINUTES AGO!!
WHAT MAKES YOU THINK YOU CAN WIN ALL OF A SUDDEN?!
BUT LET ME TELL YOU ONE THING!!
!

LIFE ISN'T ALL THAT BAD!
LEAVE ME ALONE!!!
SO WHAT IF YOU CAN FLY?!
I'M A SNIPER! I DON'T CARE IF YOU'RE FLYING OR DANCING!
HMP!!
ALLOW ME TO EXPLAIN... MY NEW WEAPON, KABUTO...
...FEATURES FIVE PIVOTS FOR ADDITIONAL STABILITY AND DISTANCE TARGETING!!
WITH THE BREATH DIAL I GOT AT SKY ISLAND, I CAN ACTIVATE IT AT THE PRECISE MOMENT I TAKE MY SHOT...
...AND SPIN THE AMMO SO IT CURVES ANY WAY I WANT! THIS SUPER SLING-SHOT IS CAPABLE OF ALL THAT!!
PING!!
KABUTO
ZOOM
BY INTERCHANGING THE FLAME, FLASH, AND IMPACT DIALS, I CAN MAKE THE SHOTS EVEN MORE POWERFUL!
NO ONE CAN ESCAPE THE WRATH OF THIS WEAPON!!!
NOW PREPARE YOUR-SELF...
SHE'S GONE!!!
WHERE'D SHE GO?!
HORO HORO... RIGHT BEHIND YOU.
?!

TRY AND HIT ME.
HORO HORO HORO...
AAAH !!!
BUTTERFLY METEOR!!!
WHY, Y-YOU... SPECIAL ATTACK...
BAM!!!
WHAT? HUH?!
WHAT ARE YOU?!
HORO HORO HORO...

SWOOSH!!
BOOOM!!
SHWINK!!
!!
YOU LITTLE...
HORO HORO HORO...
...?!!
SHE'S BACK TO HER ORIGINAL SIZE!!
I'LL SHOOT YOU DOWN!!
MANTIS METEOR!!!
KA
BOOM!!
HORO HORO HORO...
!!

?!!
WHAT...
SHNK...
...!!!
GAH!
AAAAHH !!!
HUFF
YOU STABBED 'EM RIGHT THROUGH ME! I'M FINISHED NOW...
AAAAAA
GAH! HUFF... HUFF... I'M GONNA DIE! I'M GOING TO BLEED TO DEATH!!!
Y-YOU STUCK YOUR HANDS IN ME!!!
LOOK AGAIN, IDIOT.
?!
MY HANDS ARE INSIDE YOUR BODY, BUT YOU'RE NOT WOUNDED.

STILL, YOU'LL DIE VERY SOON.
HUFF...
...!!
HUFF
BECAUSE I AM GOING TO GRAB YOUR HEART...
...AND SLOWLY CRUSH IT!!!
BABUMP...
?!!
BABUMP...
KOFF! STOP IT!
DON'T DO IT! I'LL DIE FOR SURE!!!
YOU'RE GOING TO DIE!!
NOW SQUIRM IN PAIN AS YOU GO!!
NO! I DON'T WANT TO! STOP!!
BABUMP...
BABUMP...
BABUMP
I DON'T WANT...
HUFF...
BABUMP!!
BABUMP...!!
...TO DIE...
BABUMP!!
BABUMP!!

YOU WERE BLUFFING?!!
YEAH, I CAN'T ACTUALLY DO THAT.
HOROHORO..
KR
AK!!!
SPLAP
HORO HORO HORO! IF I COULD ACTUALLY INJURE YOU PHYSICALLY, LIKE CRUSHING YOUR HEART IN MY HANDS...
AAAAAAA
...YOU WOULD'VE BEEN DEAD THE MOMENT I PUT MY HANDS IN YOU.
HUFF... HUFF...
BABUMP
BABUMP
EITHER WAY, YOU'RE BAD FOR MY HEART!!
ALL THAT HAPPENED...
BABUA
...!!
...IS THAT MY HANDS PASSED THROUGH YOU.
ACK! A SEVERED HEAD!!
AAAAAA
YEEK!!
HORO HORO HORO...
EVEN THOUGH I LOOK SOLID...
BABUMP
BABUMP
TWITCH
TWITCH
...?!
SHKK...
...MY BODY...
...CAN PASS THROUGH ANYTHING!!!
SHKK..

SPECIAL ATTACK!!
WIP WIP WIP
VIPER STAR SIX!!!
BOOM!!
?!!
I TOLD YOU, I CAN PASS THROUGH ANYTHING.
?!!
AGH! STOP THAT! IT'S CREEPING ME OUT!!
SHK..
SHK
THAT MEANS THAT NONE OF YOUR ATTACKS ...
...CAN HURT ME.

AGH! GET AWAY FROM ME!!
GO AWAY!!!
HORO HORO...
SWAP!!
SWAP!!
HUFF... HUFF...
NOW WHAT ARE YOU GOING TO DO? NONE OF YOUR ATTACKS ARE EFFECTIVE AGAINST ME.
HUFF... HUFF...
...SHUT UP!!
YOU WERE JUST BLUFFING WHEN YOU SAID YOU COULD CRUSH MY HEART.
YOU CAN'T EVEN TOUCH ME!!
I CAN'T ATTACK YOU...
BUT YOU CAN'T ATTACK ME EITHER! AM I RIGHT, OR WHAT?!
MINI HOLLOW!!
POP POP!
POP!

SNAP!
GHOST RAP!!
SHLUP...
POP!!!
GULP
SHLUP!
?!!
A SH-SHOCK WAVE?!
...!!!
KRMB...
CHNK...!!
AAAGH! GET AWAY!!
FWAP
FWAP
RAP!!!
SNAP!
BOOF!!!
...
!!!

FWOP
FIRE BIRD STAR!!!
SH!!
...!!
UGH...
HUFF
WHY, YOU!!!
FZAK!!
HORO HORO HORO.
!!!
DASH!!
...!!
!
THIS ISN'T FAIR!!
TMPTMPTMP
I CAN'T ATTACK HER, BUT SHE CAN HURT ME?!
DANG!
HUFF
HUFF
I'M NOT GOING TO STICK AROUND FOR THIS FIGHT!!
TMPTMP

HORO HORO HORO.
BAM
?!!
HEY !!
GET OUT OF MY WAY! I CAN'T SEE!!!
WHAK
GAH !!
HORO HORO HORO.
...!!
FLUP...
KLNK...
HUFF
SHLUP SHLUP
HEEZ
ACK!!

GHOST RAP!!
SNAP SNAP SNAP!!
POPOPOPOPOPOP!!
?!!
...!!!
...!!
FLUP...
WHAT IS THIS?! I'M PITIFUL!
I THOUGHT THAT GIRL WAS WEAKER THAN ME!

TMP TMP...
?!!
KUMACY...

OOO...
BE CAREFUL. KUMACY IS STRONGER THAN THE AVERAGE BEAR!!
BWAK!!
?!!
HOW CAN THIS BE?! NO ONE IN OUR CREW STANDS A CHANCE AGAINST THAT GIRL'S POWERS!!
AND I DECLARED THAT I WAS THE ONLY ONE WHO COULD DO SOMETHING ABOUT HER!!
YOU GUYS DON'T STAND A CHANCE AGAINST HER IN THAT STATE!!
SWAK!!
OH...
OH...
KRAK!!
!!
I THOUGHT THIS WAS MY CHANCE TO HELP THEM OUT. AND RIGHT AFTER I SAID THAT, THIS HAPPENS... IT'S OVER. I'M DONE. I CAN'T WIN AGAINST THIS!
I'M GOING TO LOSE, AND THAT GIRL IS GOING TO CATCH LUFFY AND THE REST AND COMPLETELY DESTROY OUR CREW.
IT WAS TOO MUCH FOR ME TO HANDLE. I SHOULDN'T HAVE THOUGHT I COULD REALLY HELP... HELP!

SHNK...!!
OH?!
HELP ME, SNIPER KING!!!
?!!
TELL ME!!
WHAT WOULD YOU DO?!
SSK K
OHHHHH!!!
OHH!!!
SSK K
AHA!!
KUMACY!!!
HOW DARE YOU HARM MY KUMACY?! AND WHAT'S WITH THAT STUPID MASK?! ARE YOU SCREWING AROUND?!!

HUFF
HUFF
NICE TO MEET YOU. MY NAME IS SNIPER KING!!
YOU ARE MESSING AROUND! YOU REALLY THINK YOU'RE A DIFFERENT PERSON?!
HUFF... I'M NOT SCREWING AROUND!!
CALM DOWN. YOU HAVE TO FIGHT, USOPP!!
NO! SHUT UP! I CAN'T TAKE IT ANYMORE! I CAN'T WIN ANYWAY!!
THAT'S NOT TRUE. I KNOW YOU'RE THE KIND OF MAN WHO CAN TAKE CARE OF THIS!!
WHAT ARE YOU BASING THAT ON?!
NOTHING.
YOU GOT NOTHING?!
TIME TO RUN!!
DASH!!
ARE YOU GOING TO RUN AWAY?!
MINI HOLLOW!!
POP OP PO
NOW THINK CAREFULLY. THERE'S A LOT THAT SEEMS SUSPICIOUS ABOUT THAT GIRL.
YEAH... ESPECIALLY THE WAY SHE SUDDENLY GOT SO CONFIDENT!
SHE WAS RUNNING AROUND IN TERROR OF ME IN THE BEGINNING!!
SHLUP
SHLUP SHLUP

IF MY ATTACKS COULDN'T HURT HER, SHE WOULDN'T HAVE RUN AWAY FROM ME TO START WITH!
SHE COULD HAVE FLOWN AWAY OR GONE THROUGH A WALL.
BUT BACK THERE, SHE WAS RUNNING AWAY SCREAMING.
YEAH, RIGHT UNTIL THAT BEAR STOPPED ME AND I LOST SIGHT OF HER!
RAP!!
BOOM!!
KABOOM
RAP!!
!!!
WHAT HAPPENED BACK THERE?!!
ZWUP
HORO HORO HORO...
NOW THEN, I SHOULD HAND YOU OVER TO MASTER MORIA NOW.
HUFF...
HUFF ...!!
I FINALLY GOT IT!
I'M ON TO YOUR TRICKS!!
HUFF...
HORO HORO HORO...
WHAT? ARE THOSE YOUR LAST WORDS?
SHWING
ISN'T THERE A ROOM NEARBY?!

HUH?!
WAIT! WHAT ARE YOU AIMING AT?!!
THAT.
BYOONG!!
HEY!
WAIT!!
SPECIAL ATTACK !!
ATLAS COMET !!
FWA
P
BOOM BOOM!!
...!!
I FOUND IT!!!
KRMBLRMBL!!
DOOM!!!
THAT'S YOUR REAL BODY!!!

Q: Oda Sensei! When Absalom says, "You're too strict on Kumacy. Un**bear**ably strict," and stuff like that, does that imply he sucks at telling jokes?

--Kanagawa Prefecture

A: That's right. Even his jokes are transparent!!

Q: Hello, Odacchi. I'm a high school senior studying for my college entrance exams, but I can't stop reading volume 47! This question is about Absalom's wildly cute snout: did it belong to the human-faced lion that Nami saw from thecarriage in volume 46? Did they exchange faces? Is it plastic surgery?! I get it now! He was a guy who hated the way his chin looked and so he couldn't get married. I want to know the truth from you, Oda!

--Failing Student

A: I see. You've paid a lot of attention to that one feature. But I will not say anything here. It is a fact that the lion's mouth was surgically removed and stitched on to Absalom's face. But there is no proof that the lion's chin belongs to Absalom. Besides, other zombies could have had similar surgeries. I will keep my mouth shut here for the sake of the small group of Absalom fans.

Q: Dear Odacchi, I forgot which volume it was, but you said you were going to include a list of *One Piece* anime voice actors. Please do it!

--Voice

A: Oh, right. You're Voice, the one who wanted to become a voice actor. I remember that promise. I did say I was going to create a voice actor intro page. But there are many One Piece-related books that already include that kind of information. I had just assumed there was no point in me doing it myself. But I came up with another good idea! I'll make a Question Corner dedicated to questions for the voice actors! Of course, I haven't gotten permission from any of the voice actors... But it'll work out somehow! If it doesn't, I'll come up with answers on my own! (?) The questions submitted for this Question Corner should be directed to voice actors who play the Straw Hat Pirates. These guys know how to take a joke, so go ahead and write anything.

Luffy: Mayumi Tanaka Zolo: Kazuya Nakai Nami: Akemi Okamura
Usopp: Kappei Yamaguchi Sanji: Hiroaki Hirata Chopper: Ikue Otani
Robin: Yuriko Yamaguchi Franky: Kazuki Yao

Chapter 466:
CONCLUSION

ENERU'S GREAT SPACE MISSION, VOL. 31:
"THE DARK UNDERGROUND CITY"

HUFF... I CAN SEE YOU CLEARLY, YET YOU CAN FLY...
...AND WALK THROUGH WALLS AND PEOPLE.
YOU CAN ALSO CHANGE YOUR SIZE AT WILL...
...LIKE A GHOST!!
...
BUT SINCE YOU RAN FROM ME AT ONE POINT...
...YOU MUST'VE BEEN IN YOUR REAL BODY AT THAT TIME!!
SO YOU MUST BE A GHOST DUPLICATE THAT WAS CREATED...
...THE MINUTE I TOOK MY EYES OFF OF YOU!
THE ONE HIDING THERE IS YOUR REAL BODY!! YOU CAN'T TRICK ME ANYMORE!
ZWOOO
...!!

DOOM!!
HMPH! I THOUGHT YOU WERE JUST SOME PESSIMISTIC IDIOT...
DID YOU GATHER UP YOUR COURAGE WHEN YOU PUT ON THAT MASK?
I'M SURPRISED YOU EVEN KNOW HOW TO USE YOUR BRAIN! BUT YOU'RE ONLY 90 PERCENT RIGHT.
I'M NOT A GHOST THAT MY REAL BODY IS CONTROLLING.
MY SOUL CAN ESCAPE FROM MY BODY...
...MAKING ME A GHOST WITH MY OWN WILL!!
I SEE!! SO WHAT DO YOU THINK WILL HAPPEN...
...IF YOU LOSE THE BODY YOU'RE SUPPOSED TO RETURN TO?!
?!

I KNOW I CAN HIT THAT TARGET!
FWAP...!!!
BIG BANG STAR!!!
?!!
HEY, STOP!!!
SMACK!!
!!
...!!
THAT WAS TOO CLOSE! WELL, IN ANY CASE YOU MISSED, AND IT WAS A DUD.
UGH!!
HUFF
FWOIN
THEN HERE'S ANOTHER!

PO
OH NO YOU DON'T! SPECIAL HOLLOW!!!
?!!
P
WHOA! SO THESE ARE LIKE THE ONES I SAW EARLIER...
...BUT SUPERSIZED?!
CHOMP!!
AAIGH!!
YOU STAY RIGHT THERE! I'M NOT GOING TO LET YOU HURT MY REAL BODY!
ZWOOP!!
POP!!
AAAA AAAA!!
FWASH!!
FWASH!!
H-HEY... WAIT! IF THE SMALL ONES CAN GENERATE SUCH A HUGE SHOCK WAVE...
...AN EXPLOSION COMING FROM ONE THIS BIG...
...COULD BLOW MY BODY INTO PIECES!
YOU WON'T BE ABLE TO TOUCH IT, NO MATTER HOW HARD YOU TRY. THAT'S THE WAY GHOSTS ARE.

BABUMP...!!
...
SWINK...!!
HORO HORO HORO! YOU WERE CLOSE, YOU NEGATIVE NEGA-NOSE!
UGH!
WITH THE SNAP OF MY FINGERS, YOUR BODY WILL BE BLOWN TO BITS!
KAMIKAZE RAP!!!
SNAP!!
...!!
ZIP...
?!!
WHAT?! IT DISAPPEARED!
HUFF ...?!
SIZZ...
DOOM!!
HUFF...
THAT WAS TOO CLOSE!
I STUFFED THE EXPLOSION INTO THIS DIAL!!
HUFF...
HUFF...
?!

WHAT DO YOU...
SKRIK!!
HUH?! I CAN'T MOVE!!!
EEK
?!
THAT "BIG BANG STAR" I SHOT...
...WAS A TRICK! IT WASN'T A DUD AT ALL! IT WAS ACTUALLY A STICKY STAR!!
I USED IT SO THAT YOU WOULDN'T BE ABLE TO MOVE EVEN WHEN YOU WENT BACK TO YOUR OWN BODY!!
WHAT?!!
NOW I CAN TAKE OUT YOUR BODY AND YOUR GHOST AT THE SAME TIME!!!
NO!!
HUH?
ARE YOU THE ONE WHO PURIFIED CAPTAIN KUMACY?!
?!
PERFECT TIMING!
GET HIM, LIEUTENANT HIPPO GALLANT!!

DOOM
IMPACT !!!
?!!
AHH...
IS HE ACTUALLY REALLY STRONG?!
WHAT ?!
OW! MY ARM FEELS LIKE IT'S BREAKING !!!
KRASH!!
HIPPO GALLANT!
FWOP!
SPECIAL ATTACK!!
SHINY BLACK STAR!!

!
PLOP!!
AH!
SKRTCH
SKRTCH
AAAAAAAAAA
AAAAH!!
COCK-ROACHES!!
ALSO KNOWN AS THE ROACH STAR!!
DISGUST-ING! SOMEONE GET THEM OFF ME! HELP!!
I CAN'T GET AWAY!!
EEEK! THEY'RE GETTING IN MY CLOTHES!!
I HATE COCK-ROACHES!! I'M SCARED, KUMACY!!! WAAAAA-AAH!
SKRTCH SKRTCH
OOOOOOO

KA BOOM!!!
YOU MIGHT BE SCARED OF ROACHES...
...BUT YOU SHOULD BE MORE FRIGHTENED BY...
...HOW MUCH YOU UNDERESTI-MATED ME.
?!!
I'M KNOWN TO BE THE STRONGEST MAN IN THE EAST BLUE.
RMB
T...
TEN TONS?! WAIT!
ULP!!
WHERE DO YOU HIDE ALL THAT STRENGTH?! STOP IT! I CAN'T ESCAPE!
I'LL DIE IF YOU HIT ME WITH THAT!!
SHK
AND GET THESE ROACHES OFF ME!!!
NOT THE HAMMER! PLEASE! NOT THE COCKROACHES, EITHER!!
USOPP'S...
I WON'T LAY A FINGER ON YOUR FRIENDS!
RMMBBB
SO, PLEASE! PLEASE STOP!!
RMM BBB
...GOLDEN...
NOOO!!!

POOOF
...POUND !!!
!!!
HUFF
HUFF...
FIZZZ...

DON'T YOU THINK IT'S JUST A BIT TOO PITIFUL FOR THE PRINCESS OF A GHOST MANSION...
SKRTCH
...TO GET KNOCKED OUT BY A BIG BALLOON AND SOME TOY ROACHES?
PLOP...
IT WAS YOUR MISTAKE...
...TO CHALLENGE ME IN A DUEL OF NEGATIVITY AND LYING!!!
DO HH!!
STAY ASLEEP UNTIL THE SUN COMES UP!!!
DOOM!!
HA HA HA HA!!

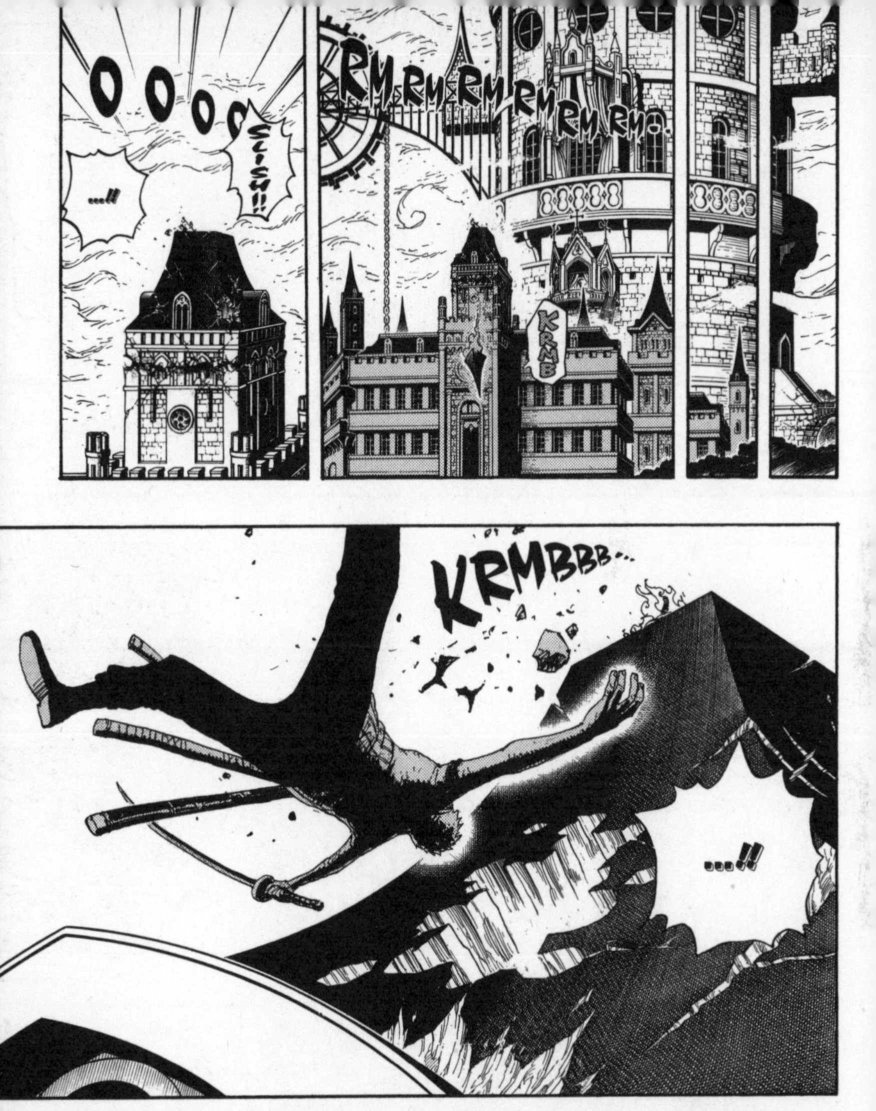
RMRMRMRMRMRMRM...
SLISH!!
OOOO
...!!
KRMB
KRMBBB...
...!!

KRASH!!!

BWASH!!
DID THAT SAMURAI JUST SAY SOMETHING?
...
SO...
HUFF
WHAT DOES THAT MEAN?
IT MEANS...
HUFF
RMRMRM..
...THE BATTLE IS OVER!!!
KRAK!
RMRMRM
I'VE NEVER SEEN A FIGHT LIKE THIS BEFORE.

DOOOM!!
KRMB...
THAT SAMURAI...
...NEVER GAVE IT HIS ALL WHEN HE WAS FIGHTING ME!
DOOM!!
WOOOOO...

FIVE MINUTES AGO, IN HOGBACK'S LABORATORY...
YO HO HO!
SO YOU WISH TO TAKE THIS BLACK BLADE...
...THE SHUSUI...
...AWAY FROM ME?!
I'LL TAKE THE SWORD THAT WILL BE LYING BY YOUR CORPSE...
...TO BE EXACT.
I SEE! YOU'RE RATHER FULL OF YOURSELF! YO HO HO HO!
I...I DON'T THINK IT'S A GOOD IDEA TO TAUNT HIM!!

I SEE YOU HAVE THREE SWORDS.
ONE OF THEM'S BROKEN.
I DON'T FEEL RIGHT WITHOUT IT, SO I STILL WEAR IT ON THE SIDE.
I USE THE THREE-SWORD STYLE.
I'VE NEVER HEARD OF THAT!
IS IT SOME KIND OF CIRCUS ACT? YO HO HO.
IT'S TOO BAD I CAN'T SHOW IT TO YOU RIGHT NOW.
I'D TAKE YOUR SARCASM DOWN A NOTCH.
I WOULD LIKE TO SEE THAT. YOU SEEM STRONG.
IT SEEMS A FEELING THAT I'VE LONG FORGOTTEN IS BEGINNING TO RISE UP AGAIN WITHIN ME.
RM RM RM RM RM...
BZZ...
BZZ...
...
IT IS AS IF I AM ABOUT TO FIGHT A GIANT BEAST...
THIS IS A STRANGE, YET EXCITING FEELING! MY BODY WISHES TO DANCE!

SHNKK
!!!
AHH! THAT SUR-PRISED ME!
KLANG!!!
CHIK...

BOOM!!
AUBADE COUP DROIT!!
KRASH!!
?!!
WHOA!
...!!!
WAS THAT A GUN?!
IT WAS A THRUST!!
BUT I NEVER HAVE THAT EFFECT WHEN I USE THAT TECHNIQUE!

COLORING PAGE!
COLOR YOUR MEMORIES WITH MERRY!

Chapter 467:
PIRATE ZOLO VS. SAMURAI RYUMA

ENERU'S GREAT SPACE MISSION, VOL. 32:
"ATTACK THE CITY FIRST, ASK QUESTIONS LATER"

HE MADE A HUGE HOLE.
KRMBL...
I DIDN'T KNOW HE COULD PROJECT HIS THRUST LIKE THAT!
HOW STRONG *IS* HE?!

YO HO HO. LOOKS LIKE WE ARE EVENLY MATCHED.
KRMMB...
...
?!

KRASH!!
!!!
WHAT?!

YO HO HO. I WAS VERY CLOSE TO BEING SLICED...
WHEN DID THE STOMACH BAND GUY HIT BACK?!
?!
ALMOST AT THE SAME TIME!!
SO HE CAN PROJECT HIS SLASHES TOO!
THE SAMURAI ZOMBIE IS MOVING RIGHT NOW WITH MY SHADOW...
...BUT WHEN HE WAS ALIVE, HE MUST HAVE BEEN A POWERFUL FIGHTER!!
IT JUST MAY BE THAT THOSE TWO...
...ARE THE SAME KINDS OF SWORDSMEN, WITH THE SAME KIND OF POWER.
WHAT'LL HAPPEN IF THEIR PHYSICAL STRENGTH IS EQUAL?
THAT MEANS THEIR DESTRUCTIVE CAPABILITIES WOULD BE IDENTICAL.
BUT THE MATCH...
...WILL BE OVER VERY SOON.

KLANGAN
PRELUDE AU FER!!
?!!
CHANK!!
IS THAT A SWORD-BREAKING TECHNIQUE?!
NIGIRI!!
CHANK!!
SH
FLASH!!
DEMON BEAR!!
SHLIIINK!!
!
WINK!!

KRAKK!!
WHOA!
ZWIP ZWIP!!
!!
WOMP
GAVOTTE BOND EN AVANT !!!
KLANK
!!
!!!

TWO-SWORD STYLE...
OOO
UNSHEATHING STYLE...
DOOM!!
CASTLE GATE !!!
HE BLOCKED IT!!!
KLINK!

!!!
THE PILLAR BROKE!!
HEY! WE'RE GOING TO GET CRUSHED!!
WATCH OUT!!
RMBB
SLIS
SH!!
HANG ON! WE'RE GETTING OUT OF HERE! THE ROOF IS COMING DOWN!!
SEVENTY-TWO POUND PHOENIX!!
BOOM!
POLKA REMISE!!
WP WP WP WP
WEAPONS LEFT!!!
KREEK KREEK...
KRAK KRAK...
SLISH!!
SLASH!!
KRAKOOM!!
BOOM!!
KRUKK!!
FWUK

HUFF
TMP!
HUFF
DMP!!
HUFF
HUFF
KOFF... KOFF...
TH-THAT WAS CLOSE!!
HM?!
KLANKK!!
!!!
GAAAH !!!
CHNNNNK
KLNK!
TUPP!!

WHOA!!
SHKKKK...
SHKKK
AHH!! WATCH OUT!! YOU'LL FALL!!
SHKKK
UGH!!
TOMP!!
HUFF
HE'S ON THE OTHER SIDE!
HUFF
HUFF
ZIP
AKLANK!!
WHOA!!
!!
WHUD!!

AHH!!
WHUK...
WHUK!!
I'M FALLING !!
WHUK!!
SHKKK
HUFF
TMP!!
DOOM!!
!
!!
HUP
KLANK!!

KLANK!!
KLINK!!
I'M SURPRISED AT HOW WELL THEY CAN FIGHT WITH SUCH BAD FOOTING...
...!!
KRMB...
HUFF...
MY SWORDS MIGHT BREAK IF THIS FIGHT GOES ON. THE BODY AND MIND OF THAT LEGENDARY SWORDSMAN LIVES ON IN HIM!!
HUFF...
HUFF...
HUFF...
CHAK...
GRP...
HUFF
...
HUFF
...
HUFF
KRMBB...

SHW AK!!
?!!
WHOA!!
HEY! ARE YOU ALL RIGHT?!!
GRIP!
TMP TMP TMP TMP!!!

ONE-SWORD STYLE!!
TUPP!!
OOOO!!
!
FLYING DRAGON ...
TMP!!
THREE-PACE...
...HUM...
!
KRMBL...
OO

NOTCH SLA... !!
!!!
ISH!!

BLAZE
!!!!

FW
ASK
?!!
GAH!!!
KOFF
THE WOUND IS CATCHING FIRE?!
BOOF
SHKK
!!
SIZZ SIZZ
FWOOO...
...!!!
...!!

...!!
HUFF
HUFF
WHAKK!!!
!!
I LOST...
HUFF...
GRP...
!
THE FAMOUS BLADE OF THE LEGENDARY SAMURAI...
HUFF
HUFF
...SHUSUI! WITH YOU AS ITS MASTER, THIS BLADE...
...WILL SURELY BE SATISFIED.
HUFF...
WOBBLE...
WOBBLE...

...
DID THAT SAMURAI JUST SAY SOMETHING?
WHAT DOES THAT MEAN?
HUFF
IT MEANS THE BATTLE IS OVER!!
I'VE NEVER SEEN A FIGHT LIKE THIS BEFORE.
THAT SAMURAI...
...NEVER GAVE IT HIS ALL WHEN HE WAS FIGHTING ME!!
IT WAS AN AMAZING BATTLE...
KLNK KLNK...
FWAP!
...
IT IS UNFORTUNATE THAT THE BODY OF THIS SAMURAI...
SIZZZ...
...MUST SUFFER A DEFEAT!!

VWOOP
SSKI
...!!
GAAAH!!
A TRUE SWORDSMAN IN MIND AND BODY...
AS LONG AS YOU FEEL SHAME, THAT'S ENOUGH.
I WISH I COULD HAVE SEEN YOU IN YOUR PRIME.
I...!!
I...
IT'S BACK!!!
PLOP...!!
MY SHADOW IS BACK!!!
...
YOHOHO
OH!!
AH!
SPLAT...!!
THE SWORD IS MINE TO KEEP!!
BUT LET'S PRETEND THIS FIGHT NEVER HAPPENED...
...SAMURAI OF THE WANO COUNTRY!!!
DOOM...

Q: Mr. 4's gun, Lassoo, has the Mutt-Mutt Fruit, Dachshund model. On the other hand, Jabra of CP9 has the Mutt-Mutt Fruit, Wolf model.
I thought no two Devil Fruits were the same. But in instances like this, different "models" of a fruit exist?

--Human-Human Fruit Model "Cute Girl"

A: Actually, Zoan-type fruits in different "models" are more like different fruits entirely. It's like this with the Mutt-Mutt Fruits, and in the case of the Ox-Ox Fruit, Dalton has the Bison model, while Kaku has the Giraffe model. Please think of them as completely different fruits.

Q: Hellooooooo! I've got a serious question despite the Question Corner's reputation for lowbrow jokes! In volume 46, Usopp said that there are no two powers that are the same in this world. But this seems to be a bit different from what was being said in a question corner in volume 45. Since the Gum-Gum Fruit is in the encyclopedia, that means the one Luffy ate couldn't be the first one of its kind! Beautiful and intelligent Eiichiro Oda, please clarify this for me!

--Takafi

A: You're pretty sharp. But it's okay. I haven't said anything contradictory. Here's a hint for you: I'll put what Usopp said in a slightly different way. "In this world, no two powers exist at the same time." Is that easier to understand? There is a certain scholar who will appear in the upcoming story who will explain what the Devil Fruits are. Soon.

Q: Hello, Oda Sensei! This may be sudden, but I found a great discovery! In the ○○○ of the ○○○○ of volume 46, the person who comes out of the snake is Yurusumaji Mask from your *One Piece* illustration book, *Color Walk 2*.
Who exactly is he? Please tell me!

--Hiromu

A: H-hey! Don't say too much! You'll put yourself in danger! He might try to kill you if you keep talking... But I'll at least tell you this: he's Pandaman's rival! He's in the employ of the Tomato Gang! Bye, Question Corner! See you next volume!

Chapter 468:
PIRATE CHOPPER VS. MYSTERY MAN HOGBACK

ENERU'S GREAT SPACE MISSION, VOL. 33:
"REVITALIZING ENERGY IN THE ANCIENT CITY"

FO HO HO HO!!!
DOOM!!
HOW DO YOU LIKE BEING HELD BACK BY YOUR CREW'S POWERS?!
YOUR SONG
HMPH. YOU TRIED TO USE SOME WEIRD MAGIC TO FEED ME SALT.
I'LL HAVE TO KEEP MY EYES ON YOU, WOMAN.
HUFF
HE'S STRONG!!
DANG, I DIDN'T THINK THAT SANJI...
...WOULD TRY TO KICK ROBIN TOO.
HE'S JUST NOT SANJI ANYMORE.
WHO'S THAT SANJI YOU'RE TALKING ABOUT?
I'LL GUT YOU LIKE A FISH, YOU LITTLE JERK!

FO HO HO! UNFORTU-NATELY...
...THEY DON'T EVEN REMEMBER A SPECK OF THE TIME THEY WERE ON YOUR CREW!
RMRMRMRM RM
THOUGH ZOMBIES IN THE INITIAL STAGES WILL RETAIN SOME OF THEIR ORIGINAL EMOTIONS...
...ONCE THEIR BODIES AND SHADOWS HAVE FULLY FUSED...
...THEY DO NOT HAVE AN IOTA OF HUMANITY LEFT IN THEM.
AS ZOMBIES, THEY CAN DO NOTHING BUT FOLLOW MY ORDERS LOYALLY!!!
TO ZOMBIES, ORDERS ARE ALWAYS ABSOLUTE!!
FO HO HO
NOW, CINDRY! FINISH THEM OFF!!
YES.

...!!
WHEN YOU'RE ACTING SO EVIL...
...I CAN SEE CLEARLY WHAT KIND OF PERSON YOU ARE, HOGBACK!!
HMM?!
IN THE PAST YOU SAVED SO MANY LIVES...
...I USED TO RESPECT YOU AS A DOCTOR.
AND IN YOUR ZOMBIE RESEARCH...
...DEATH COMES SUDDENLY, SO FOR THE DEAD AND THOSE LEFT BEHIND...
...THERE ARE MANY THINGS LEFT UNSAID. NO ONE EXPECTS THEM TO COME BACK...
...AND LIVE ON FOR SEVERAL MORE YEARS.
IT'S AMAZING IF THEY CAN LIVE AGAIN FOR ONLY A FEW MINUTES!
EVEN THOUGH PEOPLE MIGHT DENOUNCE YOU, AND CALL YOU A MAD SCIENTIST...
IF THERE IS A WAY TO REVIVE THE DEAD...

THAT'S WHY WHEN I HEARD YOU WERE CONDUCTING RESEARCH ON REVIVING THE DEAD...
...I THOUGHT ABOUT WHAT A GREAT DOCTOR YOU ARE.
...
SHWINK...
...IT WOULD MEAN SO MUCH TO THE PEOPLE YOU COULD REVIVE.
FO HO! THAT'S ABSURD. WHY WOULD I GO TO SUCH LENGTHS FOR THOSE PEOPLE?!
IT'S BEEN THE SAME ALL MY LIFE--I'M SIMPLY A GENIUS!
I PRACTICED SURGERY FOR MONEY, BUT ALL THOSE ANNOYING PATIENTS JUST KEPT ON COMING TO ME...
...INCESSANTLY, FROM ALL OVER THE WORLD! "PLEASE SAVE MY FATHER!" "PLEASE SAVE MY CHILD!"
IT WAS SUCH A PAIN!!!
I COULD SAVE THE LIVES OF THOSE WHOM NO OTHER DOCTOR COULD TREAT!!
NOW CAN YOU UNDERSTAND WHY A MAN OF MY GENIUS IS IN SUCH PAIN?!
...!!!
GO AHEAD AND RESPECT ME, IF YOU WANT TO...
BUT YOU HAVE NO RIGHT TO BE DISAPPOINTED IN ME!!!
IF YOU THINK YOU NEED TO PUNISH ME AS A DOCTOR JUST BECAUSE OUR IDEALS DIFFER...

...YOU'VE GOT A BIG MISCONCEPTION, YOU STUPID REINDEER!!
YOU WANT TO LECTURE ME ON HOW A PHYSICIAN IS SUPPOSED TO ACT?!
I DON'T INTEND TO DO THAT ...
BECAUSE I DON'T EVEN CONSIDER YOU A DOCTOR ANYMORE!!!
THE ZOMBIES HERE... THEY'RE DEAD, BUT THEY'RE BEING FORCED TO MOVE.
THEY'RE NOT ALIVE!!!
YOU'RE MAKING A MOCKERY OF PEOPLE'S LIVES!!!
FO HO! YOU SAY TERRIBLE THINGS ABOUT ME! BUT HOW CAN YOU SAY...
...THEY'RE NOT ALIVE AFTER SEEING THEM MOVE, DR. CHOPPER?! SURELY THE DEAD...
...HAVE GAINED A SECOND LIFE THROUGH THIS MIRACLE!! WHAT POINT IS THERE...
...IN DENYING THE SIGNIFICANCE OF THIS NEW LIFE?!

LOOK!!
THWAK!!
!
FWAP!!
...?!!
NOW LICK THE FLOOR, CINDRY!
?!!
YES, DR. HOGBACK.
FO HO! ZOMBIES CAN DO NOTHING BUT FOLLOW ORDERS.
EVEN THOUGH CINDRY IS A REBELLIOUS SOUL, SHE'S BEEN REDUCED TO THIS!!
...?!!
I FORGOT THAT YOU'D SEEN THAT ROOM...
...DR. CHOPPER.
SLUP.. SLUP

THAT'S MY ROOM!!
THOSE PHOTOS YOU SAW WERE OF THE THEATER ACTRESS VICTORIA CINDRY!
I WAS IN LOVE WITH HER FOR QUITE A WHILE...
...AND I WASN'T THE ONLY ONE. HER BEAUTY CHARMED EVERY SINGLE MAN IN THE NATION!
THERE. ALL DONE.
TH-THANK YOU! I DON'T USUALLY EXPECT PATIENTS TO SEW MY BUTTONS BACK ON!
HA HA. IT'S ALL RIGHT.
WHEE
SHE WAS POPULAR, BUT SHE STAYED HUMBLE.
YAAH
SHE CARED DEEPLY FOR HER FAMILY AND WAS KIND TO EVERYONE.
BUT THAT WOMAN... I HAD ACHIEVED EVERY IMAGINABLE SUCCESS AS A DOCTOR...
...YET SHE TURNED DOWN MY MARRIAGE PROPOSAL, CLAIMING SHE WAS ENGAGED TO SOMEONE ELSE!!
SOON AFTER, I HEARD THE UNBELIEVABLE NEWS OF HER FATAL ACCIDENT...
I FELL INTO A SORT OF DEPRESSION, UNLIKE ANYTHING I'D FELT BEFORE. THEN I ABANDONED MY WORK!!

AND IT WAS THEN THAT A MAN APPEARED IN FRONT OF ME...
...MY MASTER, GECKO MORIA!
DR. HOGBACK ...
LEND ME YOUR STRENGTH!

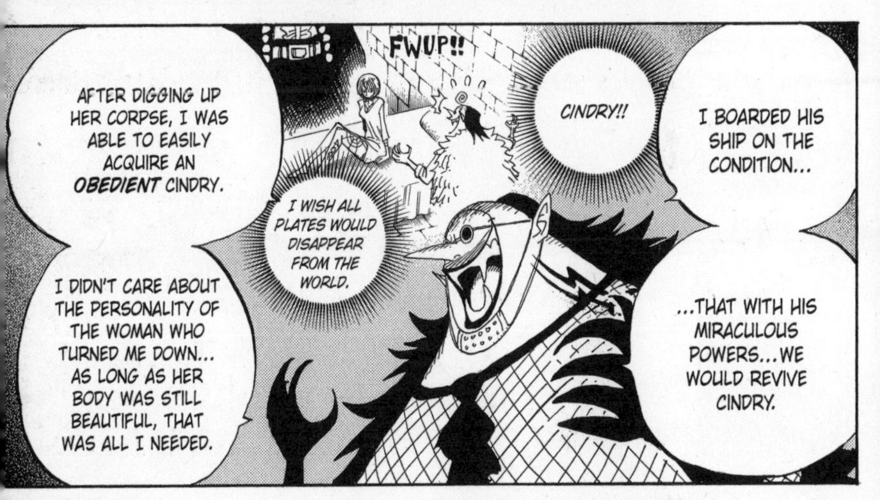
I BOARDED HIS SHIP ON THE CONDITION...
...THAT WITH HIS MIRACULOUS POWERS...WE WOULD REVIVE CINDRY.
CINDRY!!
FWUP!!
I WISH ALL PLATES WOULD DISAPPEAR FROM THE WORLD.
AFTER DIGGING UP HER CORPSE, I WAS ABLE TO EASILY ACQUIRE AN OBEDIENT CINDRY.
I DIDN'T CARE ABOUT THE PERSONALITY OF THE WOMAN WHO TURNED ME DOWN... AS LONG AS HER BODY WAS STILL BEAUTIFUL, THAT WAS ALL I NEEDED.

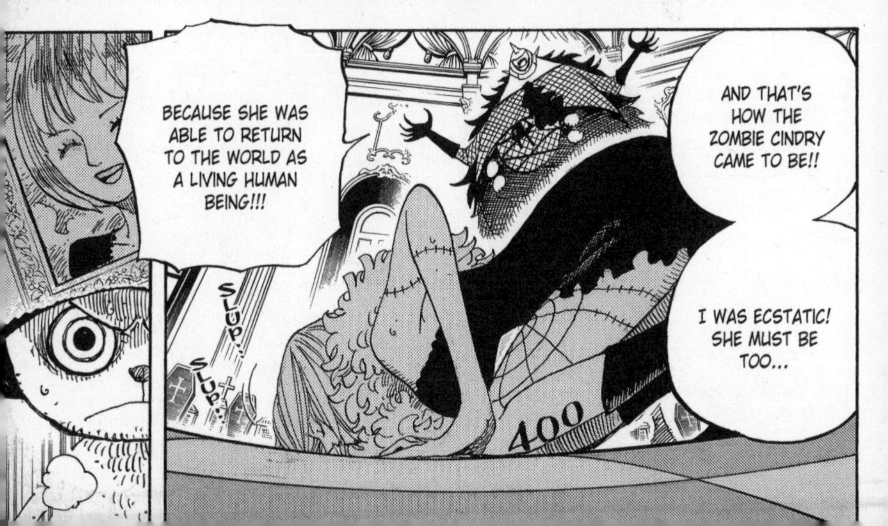
AND THAT'S HOW THE ZOMBIE CINDRY CAME TO BE!!
I WAS ECSTATIC! SHE MUST BE TOO...
BECAUSE SHE WAS ABLE TO RETURN TO THE WORLD AS A LIVING HUMAN BEING!!!
SLUP...
SLUP...
400

HOW IS SHE A HUMAN BEING?
STOP MAKING HER DO THAT!!!
?!
A CREATURE WHOSE SOUL AND BODY AREN'T CONNECTED IS NO HUMAN BEING AT ALL!!
ALL YOU'RE DOING IS USING CORPSES WITH NO FREE WILL...
SLURP...
...TO CREATE MONSTERS!!!
YOU'VE CAUSED AS MUCH MISERY FOR PEOPLE AS FOR THE MANY ZOMBIES YOU'VE CREATED!!
I FINALLY UNDERSTAND THAT! THAT'S WHY I CAN'T LET YOU GO UNPUNISHED!!!
YOU BARELY KNOW ANY MEDICINE! DON'T GET COCKY AND LECTURE ME ABOUT LIFE, PIRATE REINDEER!!!
KILL HIM, CINDRY!!
I'LL TURN YOU TWO INTO MARIO-NETTES!
CLANK
KLNK...
REJOICE, DR. CHOPPER! ONCE YOU ARE DEAD...
...I WILL MAKE YOU MY ASSISTANT!!!
...

SQUARE PLATE BLADE! ONE, TWO, THREE!!
VIP
VIP
VIP
GRAAAH!!!
T-MP T-MP!!
!
SLISH!!
GRAP!!
?!!
STOP!!
WHY, YOU...
KLNK
KLNK
KRAKK!!
!!!

CHOPPER!!
FO HO HO! DON'T UNDERESTIMATE HER JUST BECAUSE SHE'S A WOMAN!!
I'VE MODIFIED HER STRENGTH SO SHE'S BATTLE-READY!!
YOU DON'T HAVE TO LISTEN TO HIM!
OW!!
WHUK!
I WILL KILL YOU!!!
!!!
WHUK!!
WAP!!
!
YOU POOR THING! YOU'RE ALREADY DEAD!!
WHAT WOULD YOUR FAMILY THINK IF THEY SAW YOU LIKE THIS?!
...!!
LET GO OF MY HAND!!
YOU'RE PATCHED TOGETHER WITH THOSE UGLY SCARS, FABRICATED LIKE SOME EXPENDABLE SOLDIER!!
YOUR FAMILY WOULDN'T WANT TO SEE YOU LIKE THIS!

LET GO!!!
WHUK!! WHUK!!
...
YOU WERE BORN WITH BOTH A BODY AND A SOUL, BUT THAT SOUL DIED A LONG TIME AGO.
AND YET YOUR BODY IS BEING FORCED TO FOLLOW ORDERS!
WHUK!! WHUK
WHAK!!!
WHERE'S THE MEANING IN THAT?!!
ARE YOU GOING TO DOUBT YOUR OWN EYES?!
FO HOHO!!
JUST ADMIT IT! THIS IS THE ETERNAL DREAM OF MAN--TO REVIVE THE DEAD! PEOPLE CAN COME BACK TO LIFE!!
IS BEING ABLE TO MOVE ENOUGH?
HUFF
HUFF
HUF
HUMAN BEINGS NEED MORE THAN THAT TO BE FREE!!
YOU'RE THE ONE WHO'S NOT TREATING THEM LIKE HUMANS!!!
DOON!!
!!

SLINK...
ROBIN! USE THE SALT ON HER!
RSTL
SWP...
!
PENGUIN!! JIGORO!! HELP CINDRY !!!
DESTROY ALL WHO GET IN YOUR WAY!
WH
AK!!
!!!
OOF !!!
FLUP..!!
IT DIDN'T WORK!!
CHOPPER!!
RMMB
THREE-SWORD STYLE, ONE HUNDRED EIGHT...
B
B

...POUND PHOENIX!!!
WHOA!!
AHH! STOP IT, ZOLO!!
SLASH!!
DOCE FLEURS!!
!
FWAP!!
HM!
IT'S HER!
"DESTROY ALL WHO GET IN YOUR WAY!"
FWUP!!
!
SWSH!!
HEY! WHY ARE YOU ATTACKING ME TOO?!
KRASH!!!
DON'T GET IN MY WAY!!
UGH!!
KLANK!!!

DOOM!!
YOU'RE IN MY WAY! MOVE IT!!
NO, YOU!!
!
NO, ME!!
THAT ORDER TO DESTROY ANYONE WHO GETS IN THE WAY WAS MEANT FOR ME!!!
...
WHY, YOU!!
...!!!
HEY! WHAT ARE YOU TWO DOING?!
WHAKKA!! KR
AKKA!
KLANK!!
STOP IT! YOU HAVE TO COOPERA...
ROBIN!!!
!!!
BLUB!!
FLEUU
SURE.
UGH!

THIS FIGHT IS GETTING GOOD.
I WONDER WHAT WILL HAPPEN IF THEY KEEP GOING WITHOUT ANY ORDERS.
?!!
EVEN THOUGH THEY DON'T HAVE ANY OF THEIR OLD MEMORIES...
...THOSE TWO JUST CAN'T GET ALONG!!
KABOOOM!!
GRAAAAAH!!
THEY NEVER CHANGE...
...!!
FWMP
MMRM!
THIS TOWER SEEMS REALLY TALL. WHY HAVEN'T YOU TOLD ANY OF US TO JUMP OFF THE EDGE?
PHEW! WHAT?! ARE YOU ALL RIGHT IN THE HEAD?!
HUFF
HUFF
WIVV!
I'LL SAY THAT AS MANY TIMES AS YOU WANT!!
GO AHEAD AND JUMP!! BOTH OF YOU, JUMP OFF THE EDGE!!!
HUFF
HUFF

OKAY.
HUH?
KRNK!!
AAAAAAAA
WAIT!! NO! WAIT!!!
DASH!
WE'RE NOT GOING TO DO IT.
...!!!
AAAAH!
YOU WILL PAY FOR THIS!!
YOU TRICKED ME! THIS IS TERRIBLE!!
YOU PIECES OF HUMAN TRASH!!

LUFFY WILL BEAT UP MORIA AND PURIFY ALL OF THE ZOMBIES!!
KRIK!!
KRAK!!
BUT THE ONLY ONE I WANT TO BEAT UP IS YOU, HOGBACK!!!
CINDRY! BUY ME SOME TIME!!
I'M GOING TO RUN AWAY!
EEEK!!
...
HUH? ANSWER ME!!
EVEN IF YOU'RE DEFEATED, I'LL PUT ANOTHER SHADOW INSIDE YOU! JUST DIE IN PEACE!!
TOMP
TOMP
...
!
?!
MY BODY...
PLIP PLIP...
I CAN'T MOVE...
C-CINDRY ?!!

Chapter 469:
COME OUT HERE, STRAW HAT PIRATES!

ENERU'S GREAT SPACE MISSION, VOL. 34:
"CHARGE COMPLETE! THANKING THE DESTROYER!"

WHAT'S THE MATTER, CINDRY?!
DOOM!!
YOU CAN'T MOVE YOUR BODY? WHAT ARE YOU TALKING ABOUT?!
AND STOP WITH THOSE FAKE TEARS!!
FOLLOWING THEIR MASTERS' ORDERS IS A ZOMBIE'S REASON FOR BEING!!!
WHO DO YOU THINK IS ALLOWING YOUR BODY TO MOVE...
...AS LONG AS YOU HAVE A SOUL?!
THE TEARS KEEP COMING...!!
MY BODY CAN'T MOVE...

...
IT'S AS IF THE ORIGINAL OWNER OF THE BODY IS RESISTING.
BUT THAT PERSON DIED...
...TEN YEARS AGO...
CAN A SOULLESS BODY HAVE ITS OWN WILL?
THAT'S PROBABLY NOT SOMETHING...
...YOU COULD EVER REALLY KNOW, NO MATTER HOW MANY BOOKS YOU STUDY.
...!!
FWUP!!
UGH!
HUFF...
HUFF ...
!
I WILL... KILL THOSE TWO.
THAT'S RIGHT!! YOU'RE BACK TO NORMAL, CINDRY!
GOOD! NOW BUY SOME TIME FOR ME TO ESCAPE!
TOO BAD...
I WAS HOPING FOR SOME KIND OF MIRACLE.
DOCE FLEURS!!
?!!
GRA
BBAM!!
SWIP!

UGH!
BABOOM!!!
?!
WHOA!
!!
RM RM RM...
WHAT IS CAUSING THAT SHAKING?!
IT MUST BE THAT OARS AGAIN!!!
RM
RM
RM
WAIT!!
WHUPP
AAH!
AIII...
YOU STUPID PIRATE DEER!!
HOW DARE YOU PRETEND TO BE HUMAN AND TRY TO SIDE WITH THE CORPSES!!
YOU'RE NOT EVEN HUMAN! YOU FREAKING MONSTER!!
OUR CAPTAIN CAN GET MONSTERS, CYBORGS...
...BEASTS, PERVERTS, AND EXTREMELY PESSIMISTIC PEOPLE TO WORK UNDER HIM!!
HE DOESN'T NEED TO MAKE THESE VOICELESS CORPSES SUBMIT TO HIM!!!

ROBIN!!
SURE THING.
AAAAH!!!
FWIISHH!!
SPROIK
SPROIK
SPROIK
RMRMRMRM
PIERNA FLEURS!!
SPROIK
HEY, WAIT! WAIT! WHAT ARE YOU DOING, DR. CHOPPER?!
IF I FALL FROM HERE AND HIT MY HEAD...
...YOU'LL RUIN ONE OF THE GREATEST TREASURES OF MANKIND--MY GENIUS BRAIN!!
I DON'T CARE! YOUR HEAD IS THE ONLY THING MORE ROTTEN...
...THAN THESE STUPID ZOMBIES! ROBI-CHO SUPLEX!!

SAME BUILDING, SPECIAL FREEZER
SO THIS IS MY ZOMBIE?!
HE'S TWICE AS BIG AS THE GIANTS!!
KI SHI SHI. I WAS WAITING FOR YOU, OARS!!
IT SEEMS THAT YOUR BODY AND SHADOW HAVE FINALLY FUSED COMPLETELY!
HAVE YOU BECOME AN OBEDIENT ZOMBIE?
DOOM!!!
ANSWER ME! WHO IS YOUR MASTER?!
HUFF
HUFF
...
MY MASTER...
...IS MORIA!!!
DOOM!!

WHAT ARE YOU TALKING ABOUT?!
ARE YOU REALLY MY SHADOW?! DON'T LISTEN TO HIM!
WHO'RE YOU, STRAW HAT BOY?!
KI SHI SHI!!
THEN I WILL GIVE YOU YOUR FIRST MISSION!!
THE STRAW HAT PIRATES SHOWN ON THOSE WANTED POSTERS...
...
...ARE CAUSING A LOT OF TROUBLE AROUND THRILLER BARK!!
FIND THEM ALL AND CRUSH THEM!! THEN DUMP THEM BACK ON THEIR SHIP!!
IF THEY PERISH, SO BE IT! THOSE WITH BOUNTIES OF OVER 100 MILLION WON'T DIE JUST BECAUSE YOU BEAT ON THEM!!
GO AT THEM WITH ALL OF YOUR STRENGTH! SHOW ME WHAT YOU CAN DO!!!

YES, MASTER MORIA.
...
HEY! THERE'S THE STRAW HAT!
HM?!

SEE YA, STRAW HAT!
KI SHI SHI
HEY! ARE YOU GOING TO RUN AWAY?!
DASH
GUM-GUM... (EVEN THOUGH I CAN'T STRETCH)
BYOOO...
HUH ?!
...BELL !!!
HOLD ON!!!

BOOM
HUH?!
?!!
I-IT'S LUFFY'S ZOMBIE!!
OARS!!

!!!
THE FLOOR IS GOING TO GIVE WAY! CHOPPER, COME OVER HERE!
GAH!!
TOINK!!
AAAAH!
THAT WAS TOO CLOSE!
TUPP!!
...
THAT'S LUFFY?!

HOGBACK AND CINDRY FELL TO THE LOWER FLOOR!
TROMP
TROMP
GAH! IT'S TOO HEAVY!!
HUFF
HUFF
CINDRY! GET THIS ROCK OFF OF ME!!
HURRY! HURRY UP AND HELP ME!!
TROMP
...
TROMP
TROMP
OARS IS COMING!!
URK...
UGH...
I'M STUCK AGAIN!!
THIS GENIUS BRAIN OF MINE MIGHT GET STOMPED ON!!!
HEY! WHAT ARE YOU DOING JUST STANDING THERE?!
I'M YOUR MASTER!!!
TROMP!
MY BODY... CAN'T MOVE!
WHAT?!
DON'T GIVE ME THAT AGAIN!!
YOU ZOMBIES HAVE NO WILL EXCEPT TO FOLLOW ORDERS!!
HURRY UP AND SAVE ME! YOU'RE NOTHING BUT A STUPID CORPSE--YOU CAN'T DO ANYTHING BUT LOOK PRETTY!!!
...
SWIV...
...
!

GRIN
OARS! LOOK OUT BELOW! IT'S ME, YOU UNGRATEFUL OAF!!!
OARS IS COMING OVER HERE!!!
HEY!! HURRY, CINDRY!!
RMRMRMRM
...
KR MBL
!
HUH?
STOMP!!
AAAAAAAA
AAAAIGH ...
I'M THE ONE WHO MODIFIED YOUR BODY SO YOU CAN MOVE!
HEY! AAAGHH !!

SAME BUILDING, HALLWAY TO PERONA'S ROOM
HEY, HEY! WHAT'S GOING ON?!
THIS IS COMPLETELY DIFFERENT FROM THE EARLIER SHAKING!
RM RM RM RM RM RM RM RM
TMP TMP TMP...
THERE'S SOMETHING WRONG WITH THE CEILING! WHAT'S GOING ON?!
KRAKK
AAIGH!!!
IT'S THE LUFFY ZOMBIE!!!

SAME BUILDING, CHURCH
RMRM RMRM..
KRMBL!!
KRMB!!
YOU GOTTA BE KIDDING ME.
WHAT'S THAT SHAKING?!
KRAK KA!!
AAAH! IT'S A FOOT! IS THIS...
...LUFFY'S ZOMBIE?!!
ZZ ZZ
NAMI! THIS IS NO TIME TO BE SLEEPING!!
ZWIP...
WE BETTER GET OUT OF...
?!

HUH?!
NAMI?!
WHAT THE...?
NAMI DISAPPEARED! HUH...
WHY?!
THE TABLES HAVE TURNED!!
HUFF HUFF
GROWR!!
IT CAN'T BE...
YOU'RE STILL ALIVE, BEAST MAN?! SHOW YOURSELF!
OARS HAS FINALLY...
...FALLEN UNDER OUR CONTROL. THE BATTLE IS OVER FOR YOU.
RMRMRM
KRMB
THE BRIDE IS MINE THIS TIME!!
...!!
DANG IT, GIVE ME BACK NAMI! GIVE HER BACK! WHERE ARE YOU?!
HAVE THE ULTIMATE ZOMBIE PLAY WITH YOU! HA HA HA!!
KLAK
AAAAH !!!
!
SOMETHING EXPLODED OUT!!
THAT'S...
A ZOMBIE! IT'S LUFFY'S ZOMBIE!!

KRAKKA
AAAAH!
LOOK OVER THERE! THE TWIRLY-EYEBROWED COOK IS WITH HIM!
WHAT IS THAT THING?!
RM RM RM..
UGH...
NAMI!!!
WHAT IS THAT IDIOT COOK DOING?!

WAIT!!
HUFF
HUFF
TMP TMP TMP
KI SHI SHI! YOU'RE STILL COMING AFTER ME?!
I NEED TO DO SOMETHING ABOUT THAT BIG GUY, BUT TO GET EVERYONE'S SHADOWS BACK...
HUFF
HUFF
...I HAVE TO BEAT UP MORIA!! I WON'T LET HIM GET AWAY!!!
HUFF
THE CHURCH
HA HA HA!
BEHOLD...
I AM THE LAST ONE TO LAUGH!!
KRMBL...
THE SLEEPING DRUG SEEMS TO BE LASTING.
I'LL TAKE HER TO ANOTHER PLACE... AND WE'LL HAVE ANOTHER...
...WEDDING TOGETHER! MY QUIET BRIDE!!
HUFF
HEEZ
KOFF

IS MISTRESS PERONA ALL RIGHT?!
SHE'S FOAMING AT THE MOUTH!!
BUT SHE'S NOT HURT ANYWHERE!
BUZZ
BUZZ
CAPTAIN KUMACY AND THE LIEUTENANT CAPTAIN ARE GONE TOO! THAT LONG-NOSE!!
RM RM RM RM RM...
GET HER OUT OF HERE!! THIS ROTTEN BUILDING IS ABOUT TO COLLAPSE!!
THE SPECIAL ZOMBIE WILL GET OUR REVENGE FOR US!!!
IT'S ROTTEN DANGEROUS HERE! GET AWAY FROM THE MANSION!!
BUZZ
BUZZ
STOMP
AAAAAAA
WAH
WAH
THE SPECIAL ZOMBIE IS PREPARING TO FIGHT!
I CAN SEE HIS HEAD BEHIND THE MANSION! HE'S HUGE!!
PERONA'S WONDER GARDEN
HEY, USOPP!!
CHOPPER, ROBIN!! WE'VE GOT BIG TROUBLE!!
OUR WANTED POSTERS...
...ARE STUCK TO LUFFY'S ZOMBIE'S ARM!
...
HE'S TOTALLY AFTER US!!

AAAA!!!
STRAW
HAT
PIRATES!!!
SZ-900
OOM...!!!

COME OUT HERE!!!!

HE WANTS TO GET IN OUR WAY?!

RM-RM-RM-RM

LUFFY IS GOING TO CRUSH HIS OWN BAND OF PIRATES!!

IT LOOKS LIKE THOSE ORDERS HAVE BEEN GIVEN.

IS THE REAL LUFFY ALL RIGHT?!

YEEEEEE

WHAT IS THAT THING?!

IS IT EVEN POSSIBLE TO BEAT THAT?

RM-RM-RM-RM

CHK...

SOUNDS LIKE FUN!!!

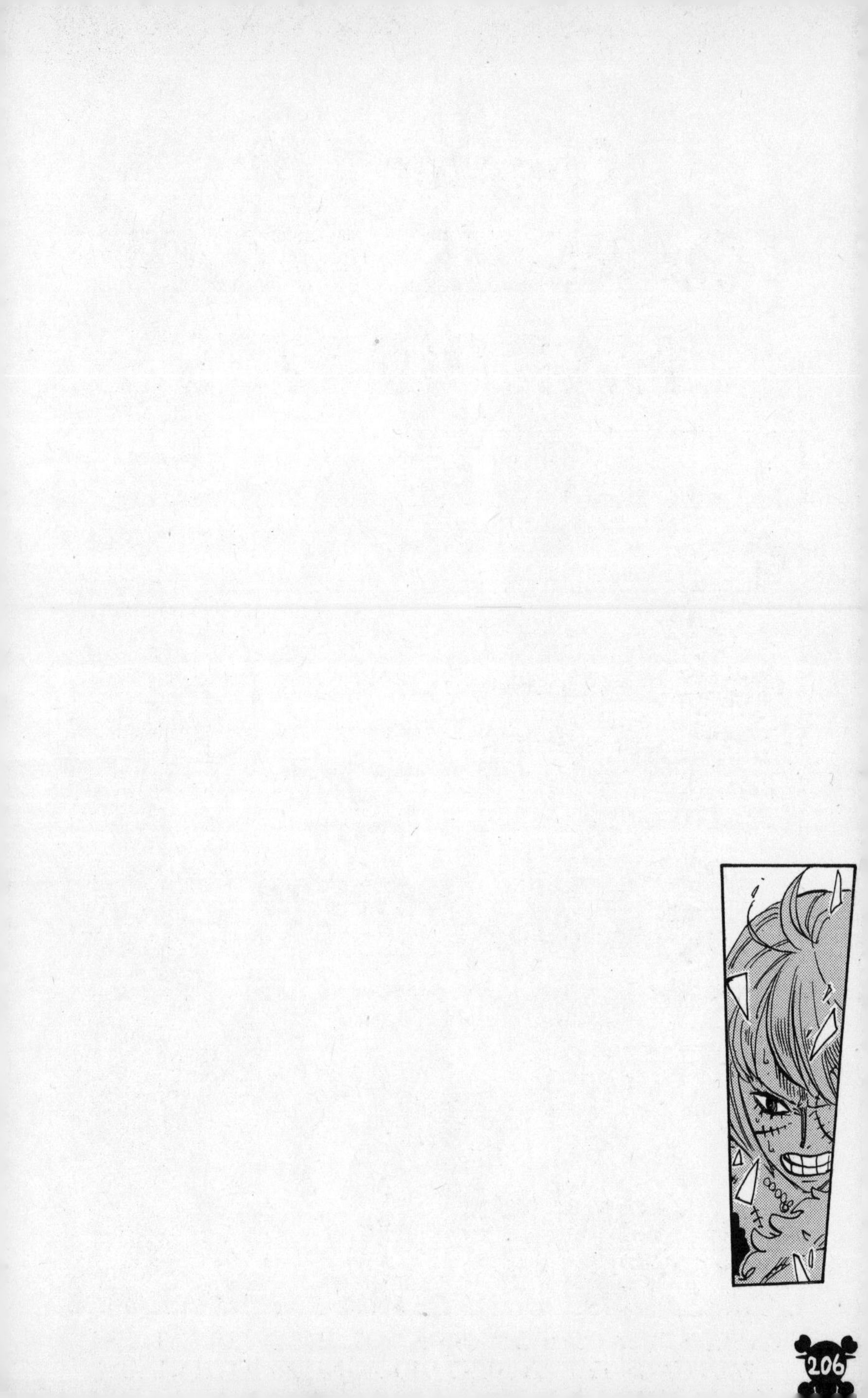

Chapter 470:

OARS VS. STRAW HAT PIRATES

ENERU'S GREAT SPACE MISSION, VOL. 35: "AN EDUCATION IN PAINTINGS: THE ANCIENT 'MOONINITES' WITH WINGS"

WAIT, MORIA!!!
RM RM RM RM RM
KI SHI SHI!!
TMP... TMP TMP TMP
WHILE YOU'RE BUSY DOING THIS...
...YOUR ENTIRE CREW IS GOING TO FALL VICTIM TO THE ZOMBIE WITH YOUR ABILITIES, STRAW HAT!! KI SHI SHI!!

USOPP! ARE YOU THERE?!
WHAT ARE YOU DOING ON THE ROOF, ZOLO?! FRANKY! BROOK!
HEY! GET OUT OF THE WAY!!

DOOM
LUFFY? THAT'S THE NAME OF MY ENEMY.
MY NAME IS OARS! NICE TO MEET YOU !!
WHY ARE YOU INTERFERING WITH US, LUFFY?!

HE'S YELLING AT THE MONSTER!
THAT STUPID COOK. DID HE RESCUE NAMI YET?
I THINK HE'S IN MORE TROUBLE THAN THAT GIRL RIGHT NOW!!
WHAT IS THAT THING?!
HIS FACE LOOKS SO SCARY !!
AAAAH
OH, CRAP! SANJI'S IN TROUBLE!
THIS IS UNEXPECTED. I THOUGHT THEY WOULD ONLY BE AFTER OUR SHADOWS.
DID WE CAUSE TOO MUCH TROUBLE?
IT LOOKS LIKE THEY DON'T CARE ABOUT ANY OF OUR SHADOWS EXCEPT LUFFY'S.
THAT'S SO SCARY! SO SCARY! I CAN'T FIGHT THAT!
WANTE
DEAD OR ALIV
SANJ
฿ 77,000,000
IDENTI-CAL... YOU'RE WITH THE PIRATES TOO!

GUM-GUM...
THAT'S LUFFY'S ATTACK!!
HE CAN STRETCH?!
DID HE BECOME A RUBBER BEAST TOO?!
...SCYTHE!!
BWAK!!
WHOA!!

HE DIDN'T STRETCH, BUT...
HIS REACH IS HUGE, AND HE'S GOT MORE THAN ENOUGH POWER!!
OARS!!
I THOUGHT I KNEW THAT NAME FROM SOMEWHERE.
COULD IT BE THE ONE FROM A LONG TIME AGO?
THE "BEAST" OARS, WHO LEFT BEHIND THE LEGEND OF THE CONTINENT PULLER?!
!
TUMP!
FWOP
COLLIER CLO...
WHAK!
!
HMPH !!!

!
WHUD!!
UGH!
!!
GAH!!
BAMM!!
THAT HUGE OAF CAN MOVE SO FAST!!
KRMBL...

GRAP!!
...!!!
THIS IS BAD! HE'S GOING TO DIE!
FIRE BIRD STAR!!!
!
BWOOF...!!

KRAKL...
...
...
OH...
FWIP
!!
AAAH!!
KRUKKA!!
!!!
AHH! SANJI!!!!
FWP FWP!!
SIZZZ...
WOOO!!
IT'S COMING OVER HERE!!!

SHOOT, FRANKY!!
GET HIS ATTEN-TION ON US!!
BAMBAMBA
GOTCHA!
?!
BAMBAMBAM...
ZWIP!!!
KABOOM!!
WHAT?!
VWEEN...
ZWIP...

AGH!!
TH-THAT WAS CLOSE!!

BOOOOM
...!!
BOTH OF YOU, GET DOWN TO ANOTHER ROOF!

DO-OM!!
ONE GORILLA...
DOOM!!
TWO GORILLA...
THREE-SWORD STYLE...
ZLA
DOUBLE GORILLA SPLIT!!!
SH...!!
...!!
ZWIP!!!
GUM-GUM...

...VOLCANO !!!
KRAAK
?!!
ZOLOOO !!
ARE YOU STILL ALIVE?! WAIT!
YOU'LL DIE IF YOU FALL FROM UP THERE!!
VEEN...
KACHIK!!!
TAKE THIS, YOU MONSTER!

BOOMBOOM!!
WEAPONS LEFT!!
TRMP!
!!
HE'S TOO AGILE! HE DODGED IT AGAIN!
AAAH!

CHANK
HUH?
NO! FRANKY !!
KRMBL...
BROOK !!!
YOHO!
KRASH!!
KRUSH!!
...!!
ZOLO IS FALLING!!!
CIEN FLEURS...
SPIDER NET!!
SWOOSH...
BWAP!!

RM
RM
RM
FWAP!!
?!!
KOFF ...!!
TAKE THIS! THIS SHOULD WORK ON ZOMBIES!!
BWAP!!
AAAAH !!!
...
DARNIT!

MUNCH!!
SPECIAL ATTACK!! SALT STAR!!!
!
...?
...
IT WASN'T ENOUGH FOR HIS HUGE BODY!!
?
HEAVY GONG!!
BWAAM!!
AAAH!
...!!!

KRMBL...
...!!!
KRMBL...
YOU...
YOU IDIOT!!
LUFFY!!
HUFF
KOFF
RM RM RM
RMRMRM...
I DON'T KNOW...
...ANY OF YOU.
KRMBL...

TO BE CONTINUED IN ONE PIECE, VOL. 49!

COMING NEXT VOLUME:

In their effort to help Brook regain his shadow from Gecko Moria and his army of zombies, Luffy, Sanji and Zolo have lost their shadows too! A human with no shadow will die if sunlight hits them… Can the crew defeat their enemies and get their shadows back before the sun rises?!

ON SALE NOW!

You're Reading in the Wrong Direction!!

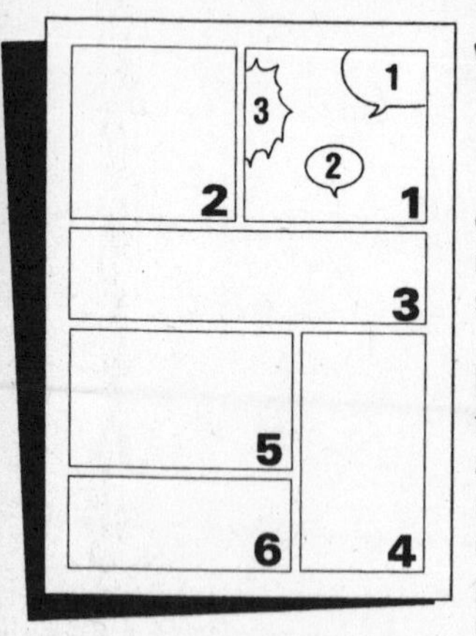

Whoops! Guess what? You're starting at the wrong end of the comic!

...It's true! In keeping with the original Japanese format, **One Piece** is meant to be read from right to left, starting in the upper-right corner.

Unlike English, which is read from left to right, Japanese is read from right to left, meaning that action, sound effects and word-balloon order are completely reversed...something which can make readers unfamiliar with Japanese feel pretty backwards themselves. For this reason, manga or Japanese comics published in the U.S. in English have sometimes been published "flopped"–that is, printed in exact reverse order, as though seen from the other side of a mirror.

By flopping pages, U.S. publishers can avoid confusing readers, but the compromise is not without its downside. For one thing, a character in a flopped manga series who once wore in the original Japanese version a T-shirt emblazoned with "M A Y" (as in "the merry month of") now wears one which reads "Y A M"! Additionally, many manga creators in Japan are themselves unhappy with the process, as some feel the mirror-imaging of their art skews their original intentions.

We are proud to bring you Eiichiro Oda's **One Piece** in the original unflopped format. For now, though, turn to the other side of the book and let the journey begin...!

–Editor